THE POOLE POTTERIES

Jennifer Hawkins

THE POOLE POTTERIES

Barrie & Jenkins
London Melbourne Sydney Auckland Johannesburg

Barrie & Jenkins Ltd

An imprint of the Hutchinson Publishing Group

3 Fitzroy Square, London W1P 6JD

Hutchinson Group (Australia) Pty Ltd
30–32 Cremorne Street, Richmond South, Victoria 3121
PO Box 151, Broadway, New South Wales 2007

Hutchinson Group (NZ) Ltd
32–34 View Road, PO Box 40–086, Glenfield, Auckland 10

Hutchinson Group (SA) (Pty) Ltd
PO Box 337, Bergvlei 2012, South Africa

First published 1980
© Jennifer Hawkins, 1980

Set in Baskerville at Input Typesetting Ltd

Printed in Great Britain by Sackville Press Ltd,
Billericay, Essex and bound by
Wm. Brendon & Son 'Ltd, Tiptree, Essex

British Library Cataloguing in Publication Data
Hawkins, Jennifer
    The Poole Potteries.
    1. Poole Pottery – History
    I. Title
    338.7′66′63942337   HD9612.8.P/

ISBN 0 09 142410 0

CONTENTS

ACKNOWLEDGEMENTS

T H I S book is based largely on interviews with employees and ex-employees of the Poole Works as this seemed to be the most valuable approach at this point. However, there is much scope for further research, for cataloguing of shapes, decoration code numbers and more paintresses' marks, for verifying and recording the vast numbers of tiling contracts and faience commissions both in this country and abroad, from Canada to India; several people are currently working on these.

I owe thanks to many people for their help in my researches. I hope that those who are recorded as interviewed in the appended lists will accept that as acknowledgement, albeit insufficient, of their kindness in providing endless information and recollections, especially David, Tony and Mrs A. Carter.

In particular I must thank one especially valuable friend, Mr William Eason, who has borne my constant questions and repeated visits with unflagging patience and rewarded me with unique details of his working experience.

Above all I must offer my most grateful thanks to Leslie Hayward, of Poole Pottery Ltd, for arranging innumerable weekend interviews, ferrying me from one appointment to the next, unearthing material from the company's records and private sources, and generally accompanying me into the convoluted history of the Carter family, the Pottery and Tileworks, with an exemplary and devoted thoroughness. No less valuable was the generous hospitality which he and his wife offered, and Sue Hayward, in addition, bore endless single-track discussions with patient fortitude.

Other help has been generous also: in particular, Geoffrey Opie typed, corrected and proof-read, uncomplainingly, for weeks; Moira Walters photographed, Barbara Morris and Paul Atterbury read parts of the typescript and advised, and Louise Irvine generously offered her own researches. All my friends and my parents supported me with considerate enquiries and encouragement.

Finally I should like to thank the management and administrative staff in Poole, London and Manchester for their interest and generosity in making available company time and records.

LIST OF ILLUSTRATIONS

1
1854-1895

From the Architectural Pottery
to Carter & Co.

WE reached the premises about three o'clock p.m. and at first sight could easily discern that something of more than ordinary interest was about to transpire. On entering the engine-room we found that the starting valve of the forty-horsepower direct acting steam engine had just been opened and the large fly wheels were making their first evolutions. The start was first-rate, every part of the machinery seemed as it should be, and all appeared right, even to a nicety, and reflected the greatest credit to the builder, Mr. James Gregory, engineer, Kingswood, near Bristol.

Early in 1855 this news item appeared in the *Poole and South-Western Herald,* reporting the official opening of the Patent Architectural Pottery in Hamworthy on Thursday 11 January. The Pottery had been established during the previous year and the report went on to describe the event in great detail:

The whole machinery of the Pottery, has been executed by Messrs. Kirk and Co., of Shelton, Staffordshire.

The contractors for the erection of the premises were Messrs. W. Curtis and G. Gollop, of Poole, and the manner to which they have executed their contract reflects the greatest credit on them. The buildings, which cover about an acre of ground, were executed under the direction of Robert Scrivener, Esq., Architect, of Shelton. The engine-house, and large chimnies [*sic*] are built of red bricks. The clay stores and other principal parts of the building are built with white and ornamented with red bricks.

Around the building were assembled, in knots here and there, happy groups of workmen, accompanied by their wives and 'fair ones', and the scene was somewhat enlivened by the presence of Case's band.

Shortly after four o'clock the Pottery gate was opened, the Company which had assembled were admitted into the yard, through which they passed to the large room of the Pottery, which is 90 feet long by 22 feet wide, and 16 feet high, which was very tastefully decorated with flags, evergreens, variegated lamps, etc. At the head of the room on a raised platform was a table, around which gathered the contractors and visitors. Immediately over the Chairman's seat was the Poole Arms, composed of perforated canvas which being illuminated had a very pleasing effect. At the end of the room on a platform was stationed the band, and on the wall was displayed in variegated lamps, the initial letters 'E.F.T.' (England, France and Turkey) over which were 'Prosperity to the P.A.P.C.' (Patent Architectural Pottery Company). Two tables which extended throughout the entire length of the spacious room were loaded with large joints of beef, legs of mutton, roast pork, hams, meat pies etc. The seats were soon occupied by about 200 guests and 'ample justice' was speedily done to the 'roast, baked and boiled'. This course having been removed it was followed by about 50 large plum puddings, and a plentiful supply of beer.

After a series of toasts in which pride and hope were expressed for the future of the new pottery, punctuated at regular intervals by 'Case's band' playing the National Anthem, *See the Conquering Hero Comes*, *Rule Britannia* and Handel's *Hallelujah Chorus*, *Cheer Boys, Cheer*, etc., Frederick George Sanders rose to speak. The news report continued:

As their Chairman had referred to the probability of His Royal Highness Prince Albert visiting the works, he might inform them that the patent itself resulted from an interview between the Prince and Mr. Ridgway, at the time of The Great Exhibition of 1851. They would, many of them, recollect the model houses then exhibited at the Crystal Palace. The articles proposed to be manufactured here would be made use of in facing houses and other buildings, and would present an improved appearance. He trusted the undertaking would be a prosperous one, and be the means of affording employment to the industrious classes.

Writing in 1878, Llewellynn Jewitt sums up the first twenty-four years of production by the Architectural Pottery.[1] 'The Architectural Pottery Company's Works were established in 1854 by Messrs. Thomas Sanders Ball, John Ridgway (china manufacturer of Cauldon Place, Hanley), Thomas Richard Sanders and Frederick George Sanders. In 1857, Mr. Ridgway retired, as did Mr. Ball in 1861, and the works were continued by T. R. Sanders and F. G. Sanders alone.' Of these men the only representative of a previously established and continuing pottery seems to be John

Portrait of Jesse Carter. c. 1890. *David Carter.*

Ridgway, of John Ridgway & Co., Cauldon Place, Shelton, Hanley, originally established in 1802 as Job Ridgway. During the period of this connection with Poole, in 1856, the Ridgway firm became John Ridgway, Bates & Co., and the name finally disappeared in 1859, two years before Ridgway's retirement from the Architectural Pottery, with the establishment of Bates, Brown-Westhead-Moore & Co.[2] Since no evidence has appeared to show that the other partners had any real experience of the industry, it seems likely that they thought it wise to include at least one member with established connections. Sensitivity, and a certain amount of personal rivalry with the Staffordshire potteries were certainly felt later in Poole and Hamworth – quite apart from the obvious commercial competition – and may very well account for the inclusion of this Hanley man at the outset.

Jewitt continues:

The productions are patent coloured and glazed bricks and mouldings, semi-perforated and pressed: patent mosaic, tessellated, encaustic, vitreous, and other glazed wall tiles; embossed and perforated tiles; quarries and fire-clay goods, etc. – the clays used being Purbeck clay, Cornish china clay, and Fareham clay, while those for plain quarries are from the Canford estate. The encaustic paving tiles are of good design, many being carefully copied from mediaeval examples. A speciality of these works are the tessellated tiles, under Bale's patent process. These are literally formed of thin tesserae of various colours, laid on and forming a part of the quarry itself. By this means all the richness and intricacy of the geometrical designs of tessellated payments are produced, and at small trouble in laying down. Their character, as a rule, is better than the Italian tiles produced on the same principle.

While the Sanders and their partners were establishing themselves in Hamworthy, Jesse Carter, the future owner of the pottery, was building up a thriving ironmongery and builders' merchant's business in Weybridge, Surrey. In the same year that John Ridgway retired, 1861, the chief technician at Hamworthy also left. This man, James Walker, set up about a mile away on the East Quay, in a three-storey building where he too concentrated on tile-making. The tiles were marked 'T. W. Walker's Patent Encaustic and Mosaic Ornamental Brick and Tiles Manufactory, East Quay Road, Poole, Dorset'.[3] The production included plain red tiles and also decorative encaustic ones, based both on the mediaeval gothic styles, which were the prototypes for the reintroduction of this inlay technique, and also on a later, Italianate, form of foliate scrolls and arabesques. In addition Walker manufactured pressed tiles in imitation of mosaic flooring, as indicated in the name of the new pottery, in the same way as his previous employers at Hamworthy. Very shortly, however, Walker's business was in financial difficulties. On 11 January 1866, there appeared in the *Poole and South-Western Herald* a notice of sale by auction of the whole of the 'Plant, Stock in Trade, Steam Engine, Pressing, Crushing and other Machines, Patent Rights etc.' with the 'Recently erected and Substantially built Pottery Premises, known as "Walker's Pottery".' No report of the actual sale appeared, however. Three years later a similar notice appeared, again with no reported sale.

Finally, in 1873, when Walker was bankrupt and the works derelict, Jesse Carter bought the pottery. Carter was then forty-three years old, his business in Weybridge was apparently flourishing, and there is no obvious reason why he decided to move into a different industry except that he was by nature a businessman with a strong belief in his own judgement. He also had some knowledge of Walker's affairs, having bought tiles from him in the past for the Weybridge business.[4] No doubt, also, he thought he could bypass any supplies problems by producing the goods himself. So, convinced that he had some chance of rebuilding the failed enterprise, he moved to Percy House, 20, Market Street, Poole.

Jesse and his wife, Mary Elizabeth Callaway, had six children: Alfred (b. 1849), William (b. 1852), Annie (b. 1854), Ernest Blake (b. 1856), Charles (b. 1860), and Owen (b. 1862). Mary Elizabeth was rumoured to have been of Italian or gipsy stock. In later years her daughter Annie, widowed after a short marriage, became a suffragette with a penchant for pipe-smoking, which some people said revealed her exotic ancestry.[5] By comparison, the father was a very active member of the Plymouth Brethren and enforcement of this demanding and difficult creed undoubtedly had its effect upon the children. Three were destined to work in the Pottery but the eldest two, Alfred and William, set up on their own. Alfred left for London soon after the move to Poole. In October 1876 he was in Nunhead running a small catering business. His young brother Charles visited him there and noted in his diary that Alfred was 'doing a roaring trade in sausages, pease pudding, etc.' Later he tried the same field as his father had done and became a builders' merchant. Eventually he opened a tile merchants' business in Brockley Rise in south-east London, and for some years struggled with serious financial problems. By that time Charles was managing the administrative side of the Poole works, and in the early 1900s would discuss these difficulties with Alfred at Brockley during his visits to London.[6]

His brother William, equally determined and independent, broke away early from the rather stifling atmosphere of the family

Group photograph, 1890–95. Left to right, back row: unknown, unknown, Alice (sister of J. R. Young), James Radley Young; middle row: possibly Polly (sister of J. R. Young), W. C. Unwin, Mrs W. C. Unwin, Alfred Eason, Mrs A. Eason; front row: Emmie (sister of J. R. Young), unknown, unknown, unknown. *Mrs C. J. N. Unwin.*

home. However, like Alfred, he was not by any means entirely divorced from what was to become the most famous of the Carter family enterprises, for he opened his own brickworks at Foxholes, Parkstone, and later, in 1884, bought the Kinson Pottery, also at Parkstone, where he specialized in stoneware piping.[7]

The first eight years at Poole were difficult. Initially Walker, a fellow member of the Plymouth Brethren, was kept on as manager. However, in 1876 he was dismissed for dishonesty, self-confessed as the cause of a discrepancy in the firm's accounts.[8] A lime kiln that had been erected on the land adjoining the three-storey building was destroyed by fire (the surviving foundations still exist and are incorporated into the craft section of the present-day Poole Pottery works). Early efforts to sell the tiles in London and around the country were of limited success. Jesse also tried further investments and, in 1880, bought at least part of the St George's Works in Worcester from David Wilson Barker. Barker had been manufacturing a wide range of wares from 1872 or earlier. The works at that time were known as the St George's Patent Brick, Pottery and Terra Cotta Works, and in 1873 Barker advertised himself as 'manufacturer of patent pressed, stock and builders' bricks; also rhubarb, seakale, chimney and garden pots, vases, seed pans, garden tiles, and all kinds of ornamental rustic work'.[9] When Jesse bought into the business, the works divided into Barker's patent Brick Works and the St George's Tileworks, owned by Carter & Co., which shared the same address, St George's Lane. By 1888 a new name appears among the Tileworks proprietors, Carter, Johnson & Co.[10] By 1892 both Carter and Johnson as well as the St George's Tileworks are no longer recorded. According to Jesse's grandson Herbert:

His agents, too, in more than one instance, proved unsatisfactory or downright dishonest and a man named Parkinson, who had put money into the business, tired of it after a few months and was paid off on generous terms, for he took the Worcester pottery and the London depot stock in trade and paid £300 for the lot. But I cannot say what became of his invested capital.[11]

Herbert Carter may have been mistaken in remembering the name Parkinson, which should perhaps have been Johnson. No mention of either Parkinson or Johnson appears anywhere in the scant Carter & Co. records of this date.

Despite these setbacks, gradually the works on East Quay over-took the successes of its rival, the architectural pottery at Hamworthy. In 1867 the Hamworthy firm was exhibiting floor and wall tiles in the Universal Exhibition in Paris. In 1878 they were advertised in the *London Business Directory*. Their London office was 11, Adam Street, Adelphi, and under the provincial appendix to the Encaustic Tile Makers' section they were entered as:

Hamworthy, Poole. ARCHITECTURAL POTTERY CO (THE) PRIZE MEDAL, International Exhibition 1862 and Dublin 1865, awarded for excellence of manufacture and beauty of design. The original Encaustic Tile Works established by the above company at Hamworthy, Dorset, in 1854. Manufacturers of encaustic, mosaic and tessellated tile pavements, including vitreous, blue, white and green tesserae for churches, halls, conservatories etc. White glazed tiles and coloured, plain and with patterns for baths, dairies etc. Sheets of patterns, prices and estimates on application.[12]

By the same year, Carter & Co. had begun to establish a foot-hold. A London office was set up at 24, Featherstone Buildings, Holborn, and under Tile Manufacturers (Enamelled and Encaustic), in the same Directory, their main entry advertised their products only five years after Jesse had bought the works.

Poole, CARTER & CO., Poole Pottery. All kinds of encaustic mosaic, marble granite and tessellated paving tiles. Also glazed tiles for hearths, walls, flower boxes and grates at lower prices than charged by any other maker. Estimates for laying if required. . .[13]

By 1880 they were competing effectively with Wedgwood, no less, whose agents complained that 'Carter of Poole do them the most injury . . . they sell thin tiles as seconds at a very low rate and thin floor tiles . . . they do fixed at a less price than they [the agents] can buy the tiles for'.[14]

In 1881 the Pottery was on a sure enough footing for Jesse to have taken his three youngest sons into the family business. Ernest Blake began by assisting with the book-keeping in London. He was never a robust person[15] and in 1883 he died of rheumatic fever, leaving Charles and Owen to become the only two members of Jesse's family to work at the Pottery. As early as April 1877 Charles was recalled from Weybridge, where he had been employed at Jesse's building business. There is no record of Owen attempting any other form of employment and it seems that he went straight into the Pottery aged about fifteen or sixteen, at about the same time as Charles. Charles' contribution to the growth of the Poole Potteries, as they became known locally in Poole and Hamworthy, was administrative. He was a talented businessman and served for many years on the Poole Town Council to which he was elected in 1888; he also served a term as Mayor. Owen was concerned with the artistic development of the production and so, between the brothers, the needs of the works were well balanced.

In 1886 Carter & Co. were fully established as an important tileworks, attracting the following comment from *The Building News*:

The rapid increase of fine art industry of late years in connection with encaustic tile and enamel ware deserves notice, as there can be no doubt that the development is due to the inherent excellence of the work itself, rather than to any adventitious aid. Foremost among the revivalists of this art is the firm of Carter and Co., of Poole, whose mural pictures can be seen in various parts of the metropolis and its suburbs, in the entrance-halls of some of the leading taverns. All the subjects they treat pictorially embody some historic or local event, and so have a permanent interest in the neighbourhood. The most recent addition to this gallery of art has just been placed in the 'Cambrian Distillery', in Cranbourne Street,

Leicester-square, an old house which has recently been rebuilt and reopened with all the modern improvements and conveniences for health and comfort. The architects were Messrs. W. E. Williams and Son, of 46, Leicester-square, and the contractor was Mr. Robt. Marr, 24, Wheeler-street, Spitalfields, E. The picture referred to illustrates a notable murder which was perpetrated in Leicester-fields in the latter part of Charles II's reign. The occasion was one which drew together as motley a group as ever delighted the artist's eye. Court gallants, in all their bravery of slashed hose and doublet, lace and ruffles, and Rembrandt hats; Puritans, who still had the courage of their opinions, as expressed in their attire; link-boys, swashbucklers, and the miscellaneous crowd of roughs of the period formed an exciting group, which the artist has done full justice to, whilst the expression on each face is life-like, spirited, and in startling contrast to the placid quietude of the corpse. The subject is a delicate one to handle in a popular manner; but the artist has succeeded in avoiding the ghastly sensationalism which is the great source of danger in dealing with such subjects. For the rest, the picture is noticeable for the harmonious blending of colours and subdued softness. The framing, consisting of flat and moulded majolica, is appropriate. This is only one of many pictures with which Messrs. Carter, however, have adorned various parts of the metropolis and suburbs, and each of these is associated with some subject of historic local interest, which is sure to attract the public. An important branch of the firm's work consists in laying mosaic flooring, with lettering inlaid, which forms an attractive advertisement. We have noticed this style of decoration fully, as it marks a new and important departure in the way of hotel decoration, and tends to develop a new revival and improvement of an old and beautiful yet erstwhile almost obsolete form of artistic work. Messrs. Carter, however, do not confine themselves to the production of *genre* subjects; they also excel in land and seascapes, noticeable for the delicate yet rich blending of colour, *chiaroscuro*; and for the more severe taste they have some splendid specimens of classical, life-sized outlines for mural decoration in monochrome. We would strongly advise architects and builders to see the work of this firm before sending out specifications. The firm will gladly supply every particular that may be required.[16]

The inclusion in its entirety of this article is intended to illustrate the success and growth of the firm only thirteen years after Jesse had bought the failing works from James Walker. Similar painted panels such as those in The Hare, Hoxton, or The Swan, Great Dover Street, were also described fully; the range of subjects included 'Old Bartholomew Fair', 'Little Dorrit' and 'Swearing on the Horns' as well as scenes taken from Poole and the Dorset

countryside[17] and clearly, by this time Carter's had far outstripped
the rival Architectural Pottery at Hamworthy in the range of tiling
produced and the extent of contracts fulfilled. They were pioneer-
ing developments in mosaic flooring, a technique in which they
continued to specialize into the twentieth century and through the
1920s and 1930s. Their moulded and decorated tiles were used
both locally and as far afield as Birmingham. The excellence of
their scenic painted panels was indisputable and the efficiency of
the marketing side of the business put them in successful competition with other major tile manufacturers of the period. In this
same year, 1886, the Tileworks were awarded a silver medal at the
Building Trades exhibition for 'Superiority in Workmanship and
Material'.[18] In 1891 they received the Prize Medal and Star cer-
tificate from the Society of Architects and in the same year their
illustrated catalogue was reviewed enthusiastically by *The Building
News*. This journal continued to report on the firm's progress,
recommending, in 1892, their 'very hard and extremely well made
Petrous tiles' in black, chocolate, red, grey and buff.[19]

In 1893 Owen contributed a chapter on tile design to a publication called *Practical Designing*. He covered the main groups:

(1) Plain geometrical floor tiling; (2) Encaustic floor tiling, alone or in
combination with Class 1; (3) Mosaic floor and wall tiling; (4) Plain,
embossed, or printed tiles, either alone or combined, for wall surface
decoration; (5) Hearth and grate cheeks; (6) Faience. Designs for all the
foregoing would be prepared by the combination of a greater or less
number of individual tiles worked together to form the pattern, which
latter may again be subdivided into (7) Encaustic floor tiles; (8) Glazed,
embossed tiles; (9) Printed tiles; (10) Painted tiles, either with a complete
design on each, or united for fireplace panels, etc., or in ceramic pictures,
illustrating historical or other subjects.

This list includes the chief varieties which are employed decoratively,
and for which really good designs in any of the classes ought to find a
ready sale. Many of the best makers, although they have competent
artists on their staff, are not averse to buying first-class designs from
outsiders, as they obtain thereby greater novelty and change; but some
of the smaller makers, of printed tiles especially, rely entirely upon outside
designing (often of a very inferior quality).

. . . In designing for these tiles the novice has more opportunity than
any other, since there is a large demand for them at the present time.
Printed tiles are made by many small firms who do not employ artists
permanently on their staff, and so most of their designs are either adapted

(in plain English, cribbed), or bought from outsiders. The price paid by the smaller makers is usually from 7s.6d. to 15s. for a 6″ tile. The purposes for which printed tiles are used are numerous. Besides being employed in the fixtures of houses, they have lately been worked into furniture, and other portable objects.

He described the wide range of sizes made in plain, geometric floor tiling, from 6 ins square to $1^1/_{16}$ ins square (in which series the largest is an exact multiple of the smallest), diagonal halves of all these sizes, strip borders and octagons. He explained that:

The cheapest colours to manufacture are buff, salmon, grey, red, chocolate and black, all of which cost about the same, and are known as 'plain colours'. White is nearly twice as expensive, and blue and green nearly three times as much. White, blue and green (termed the vitreous colours) are seldom made in the sizes above 3″ × 3″ squares, from the difficulty in keeping the larger tiles straight, owing to the vitreous or glassy nature of the body. Consequently, $2^1/_8″ \times 2^1/_8″$, $1^1/_2″ \times 1^1/_2″$, $1^1/_{16}″ \times 1^1/_{16}″$, and their diagonal halves, are the most useful and customary sizes. In preparing a design based upon these simple plain tiles, it is as well not to make too lavish a use of the more expensive colours.

Each of the main groups was dealt with in turn, giving a guide to the types of design possible with each class of tile material. Architectural faience, however, was deemed to be outside the province of the designers to whom Owen's comments were addressed. Since the book was aimed at the ambitious novice, he concluded:

We should advise anyone who wishes to take up any (or all) of the foregoing branches of tile designing to study some manufacturer's books of patterns and the actual tiles. In the matter of designing for printed tiles, it would be easy to obtain from a merchant, who would probably keep a variety of makers' patterns, a dozen or so of odd patterns (seconds) at trifling cost, which would give a better idea of the different styles than all the written information. Original and yet beautiful designs will be caught up rapidly and be well remunerated, as originality is much sought after; but, since all of us cannot expect to produce entirely original ideas, we must be content to tread in the footsteps of others, for this the illustrated specimen books will also be found of immense assistance. If in the neighbourhood of the potteries in Staffordshire, or Poole, Dorset, it is not hard to obtain permission to look over a manufactory (this will, in almost all cases, be granted to anyone not in the trade), and realise fully the process, which is the first requirement to the creation of new and good designs.

For the first effort in selling designs, remember that the smaller makers will probably be your best customers.

Distinguish between merchants and makers; the former will only require complete arrangements of designs for a floor, wall, and so on; designs of single tiles would be of no use to them as they do not manufacture; if your designs please them, they may employ you to make special designs, giving you general instructions as to what is required, and supplying you with the detail designs to use in the pattern. Hitherto designing of complete patterns has been restricted to the staff of the manufacturer or merchant, outsiders only designing for special tiles, such as single printed tiles, etc.; but we do not see that this need necessarily be so.

One word in conclusion: do not be discouraged by failure at first, but persevere, and bear in mind that to make your designing a success, from a pecuniary point of view, you must be businesslike; if you are not this, no matter how good your designs are, you will not succeed; and – don't ask as much again for your designs as they are worth, especially at first.[20]

Although there is no doubt that Carter's made all the types and sizes of tiles described, there is no firm indication in the article of the company's attitude towards outside designers. However since, from the tone of Owen's remarks, the purchase of designs was established practice for tile-makers, it seems likely that Carter & Co. bought in designs and patterns as well as relying on their own staff artists.

Unfortunately there are no documentary records of the artists working with Carter's at this period. The first painter known to have worked there is a man named Edwin Page Turner, who arrived from Sheffield at some time before 1893. In 1893 he was joined by his half-brother James Radley Young, who was destined to figure largely in the development of the Pottery. Radley Young was born in Macclesfield in 1867 and studied painting and modelling at Sheffield School of Art. He then supported himself for a while with various portrait and other commissions, and also by helping in his father's decorating business at Southport, to where the family had moved. It is probable that his older half-brother was already at Carter's and in consequence he joined him at the fast-growing firm.[21]

The East Quay works, originally constructed by Walker as a three-story building, was flanked on its south side by a row of bottle kilns, lining the harbour edge. East Quay Road today marks the original shore line, the land between that road and the present harbour edge being reclaimed soon after 1900. Over the first twenty years of ownership Jesse added his own extensions to the works in a piecemeal and somewhat eccentric style. The long wall facing the quay, still standing today, was built by him. In it are incorporated quantities of tiles and waste materials cemented together with black mortar to his own special recipe. The roof was covered with floor tiles set in pitch and supported by pit props. Repairs were effected with more tiles and pitch, regardless of the weight, and the inevitable sagging was supported with yet more pit props until the top floor was virtually a forest.[22] This precarious structure became known as the 'Pillared Hall'[23] and survived through two world wars; all but the long south wall was demolished in 1946.

After their successes in the 1860s and 1870s the Architectural Pottery gradually lost its lead over the new works at Poole and by 1895 Jesse Carter was in a strong enough position to be able to buy out the Architectural Pottery's 'very extensive works'.[24] The forthcoming auction was announced in the *East Dorset Herald* on 26 September 1895. The property included 'Five Freehold Cottages, 56 Plots of Ripe Freehold Building Land' as well as the Pottery itself and the land on which it stood, all part of the Hamworthy building estate. It seems that it was decided to sell the Pottery at the same time, probably rather than risk an increase of ground rent or other costs under a new landlord at a point when, presumably as a result of the nearby competition, their fortunes were at a low ebb and mention of them in contemporary journals had disappeared. The sale took place on 17 October and Jesse and Charles Carter bought the works for £2,000. With this purchase Jesse then owned the two sites which became known as the Poole Potteries and which, with much expansion and development, acquired a distinctive style and a ready and dedicated market, both for its tile production and its domestic and decorative pottery.

2
1895-1914

Tileworks, architectural faience and lustre glazing

IN acquiring the Architectural Pottery the Carters bought a connection which had great significance for the artistic side of the firm's development. William De Morgan had been buying tile blanks from the Architectural Pottery since the early 1870s. He had begun decorating tiles and pottery in the 1860s and in 1872, when he moved to Chelsea, he began experimenting with lustre glazes in earnest. At first he bought tiles, and then during the 1880s he began to purchase bowls and dishes. This he continued to do until after 1900 and so was in contact with the Carters at least on a business level for about ten years. The Victoria and Albert Museum owns a bowl with the impressed signature and date 'Carter, Poole 2/1904', probably decorated by Charles or Fred Passenger to designs by William de Morgan. The bowl is part of the bequest made to the Museum by De Morgan's widow. In the light of developments at Poole it seems probable that the Carters, particularly Owen, were aware of, and sympathetic to, the use made of their blanks by the artist-designer.

Owen Carter was also an artist – a talented painter in watercolours – and was keen to improve the artistic side of the firm's output. Around 1880 Jesse Carter moved from Market Street to West End House, by St James' Church, and this had been the family home while his children were growing up.

By his retirement in 1901 he had moved to Bournemouth.

Panel of tiles painted with lustred red glazes, set into a wall at the East Quay works. c. 1903–4. *Photograph: Pilkington Tiles Ltd.*

Around 1900 Owen began those experiments which were to lead to a new branch of the parent firm. He had moved into West End House and in the stables he learnt to throw on a wheel and began taking his bowls and vases into the works for glazing and firing.[1]

Glazing was his particular interest and he concentrated all his efforts on the technique of reduction firing to produce a range of lustre glazes. An account of the method as it was employed in the 1920s at the Tileworks probably illustrates Owen's own practice fairly accurately. He had constructed, at the Architectural Pottery works, a small coal-fired muffle kiln, only five or six feet in diameter, specially for the firing of the lustre-glazed wares. He used a soft lead glaze containing silver chloride for blue, grey or green effects and copper for a range of reds and purples. A clear base glaze containing a little of either of these minerals was sprayed on and the piece fired at 1000 – 1020°F. It was then resprayed with a mixture of china clay and silver or copper and fired again at a maximum temperature of 800°. The kiln had a false floor in the form of an iron grid (probably constructed from old mill pan bottoms, used for grinding colour powders), under which were pushed old leather, wood and other materials to reduce the atmosphere. The kiln was then left to cool and this process fumed the glaze. The test pieces were taken out and wiped at intervals while cooling down – at 700°, 650° and 600° – to see if they had lustred successfully and to ensure that the atmosphere was being maintained during the reduction. After that point more oxidizing conditions were considered to brighten the lustre effect. Since conditions throughout the kiln varied in atmosphere and temperature, part of the contents of the kiln would be lustred and part not, so it was usual to empty the kiln, clean off, reset the contents and repeat the final firing.[2]

In these experiments Owen worked closely with James Radley Young and Alfred Eason. Radley Young had developed his own lustre glaze recipe which he eventually sold to Carter's in an uncharacteristically shrewd move. Alfred Eason was a very experienced man, originating from Stoke-on-Trent where he had worked for Spode and Minton. He emigrated to America for a while where he was employed with the American Tile Company, producing encaustic and relief-moulded tiles of excellent quality. He returned to England and, since his wife's health meant that they had to live in the south, he started at Carter's in 1888. He was the chief glaze

Design for a staircase, illustrated in *Leadless Decorative Tiles, Faience and Mosaic* by
William J. Furnival. *c.* 1904.

man and works manager for many years, certainly during the First World War, and was responsible to a large extent for the glaze experiments and developments during that time.[3]

Owen himself also studied the chemistry of glazing and firing techniques. He bought the most recently published studies on the subject and two of these publications survive, signed by him on the flyleaves and with various annotations. The first is *The Chemistry of Pottery* by Karl Langenback (Superintendent of the Mosaic Tile Company, formerly Superintendent of the Rookwood Pottery, and Chemist of the American Encaustic Tiling Company), published in America in 1895 and in Owen's possession by 1897. The notes in this book are in connection with the separation of the clay constituents, glaze analysis and cream-coloured ware. The second book is Volume 1 of the *Collected Writings of Hermann A. Seger*, again an American book, this time bought by Owen in the year of publication, 1902. Seger was Professor at the Royal Technical Institute, Berlin, and Chief of the Chemical-Technical Experiment Station, the Royal Porcelain Manufactory, Berlin. He also developed Seger cones, used in judging kiln temperatures. His book covers all aspects of clay, drying, glazing and firing. Since both books are American it seems possible that they were bought at Eason's recommendation. Although one cannot be certain that the annotations are Owen's, the books do not appear to have been in regular use by more than one person and the very fact of his ownership is evidence of serious study. Also, Owen is known to have been in correspondence with William Burton on the subject of lustre glaze recipes. Unfortunately this correspondence, until recently in the Pilkington records, is now no longer available. However, there are copies which were made in the 1930s of earlier body and glaze ingredients, which may have been the recipes discussed. Certainly there are close similarities in the appearance of many of the lustre glazes, particularly the reds, used by the two potteries. The Carters also kept abreast of contemporary movements in the decorative art world. In 1900 Charles and Owen went to Paris and spent five days at the International Exhibition in which the *Art Nouveau* style reached its pinnacle of extravagance and effect.[4] After the turn of the century, from about 1901 onwards, the production of lustre-glazed vases, candlesticks, dishes, jardinières and so on, was recognized as part of the firm's output. There is one exception to the otherwise unanimous opinion that the lustre

wares were always fired at Hamworthy. A tile decorator remembers working at Hamworthy during the First World War. At intervals she was called upon to accompany Harry Jones, the glaze-
maker and dipper, to Poole with a consignment of pots made at
Hamworthy by Lily Gilham. These were lustre-glazed and fired at
Poole and it was her job to clean off the excess glaze before firing.[5]
It is possible that the extraordinary circumstances of war-time
brought about a change in the established procedure, for in the
heyday of lustre production it seems certain that this specialized
firing was all done at Hamworthy. Among the surviving records
a cash book exists in which are noted some details of firings from
March 1900 to December 1908. The glost firing of pots is first
mentioned in December 1900 when 84 pieces were fired at Hamworthy. These firings are recorded regularly, almost monthly, at
intervals up to July 1908. The largest number fired in the first year
was 134, in September, and the highest number fired in one kiln
over the whole period was 214, in January 1905. Generally the

Painted panel at Hooper & Son, fish shop, Southsea (from a contemporary
photograph). *c.* 1910. *Pilkington Tiles Ltd.*

entry is limited to the number fired (although even this is frequently unspecified) and the minimal identification 'pots'. In June 1906 the entry is simply 'lustres', with no identification of the type of ware. In February 1907 it is recorded that 19½ yards of lustre tiles were fired. The entries, although regular, are in the form of a supplement to the main record of glaze kiln firings of tiles. Other wares fired at the same time are noted in the same brief manner as the pots and include faience, which was biscuit and glost fired at both Poole and Hamworthy; bricks, briquettes, fireplace sets, roofing tiles, saggers and cranks (Carter's made all their own kiln furniture), all of which were fired at Hamworthy. There is no record of pots sold, unfortunately.

In July 1901 a second building and site was purchased at Hamworthy, on the other side of the Blandford Road. This works had been used for the manufacture of whiting and had therefore been known as the Blue Works, referring to the blue used in that process. Confusingly, under the Carters it was put to producing white and

Painted panel at the Nelson Arms, Merton, surrounded with glazed faience. 1910.
Pilkington Tiles Ltd.

cream-glazed tiles for which there was a rapidly increasing demand. As a result it became known as the White Works.[6]

The two tileworks at Hamworthy were becoming increasingly important and productive, as the White Works gradually caught up with the well established Architectural Pottery works. In March 1903 recorded values for fire insurance purposes stood at £7,970 for Poole, £4,425 for the A.P. and £4,000 for the new White Works, or W.W. as it became known. Stock and equipment are not mentioned in this record. In 1900 *Architectural Pottery* by Léon Lefèvre was published in England, and while finding it 'impossible to mention all the important houses making incrusted quarries in England', he nevertheless named a shortlist of five: 'Among the best known are: Messrs Carter & Co., Doulton & Co., Maw &

---

18 March 1903

Packing. In casks or Boxes 4d yd. Trucks 1d yd.
Seconds

White vitreous		5/-
Plain Floor Tiles all colors from 6″ × 6″		
to 3″ × 3″		2/2
Black under 3″ × 3″		2/8
Other colors under 3″ × 3″		2/6

If we cannot supply above in Seconds we undertake to do so in Unselected or even Best at same prices.

	Best	U/S	Secs
Enamels	6/10		6/-
Skirtings	8/-		6/10
Plain Capping & Mouldings	9/-		7/9
Brick Pattern Embossed	7/6		6/10
Blue & Green Vitreous	10/3	9/-	
Sage Green Vitreous	8/-		
Encaustic	6/6		5/-
3″ × ½″ Enamels	10/-		
1″ × 1″ Black	3/-		
1″ × 1″ White	6/9		

Faience and painted panel made for the Manchester office building, the sculptural work almost certainly by W. C. Unwin. 1905. *Mrs C. J. N. Unwin.*

Co., Minton, Hollins & Co., Woolliscroft & Son, etc; all of them produce pieces which are excellent both in quality and ornamentation.'[7] Carter's themselves kept a note of the types of tiles made and lowest prices allowed for their standard production.[8]

By 1904 W. J. Furnival, writing on the 'Rise of the Modern Industry – Modern British', devoted several paragraphs to Carter & Co.'s tile production, based on an interview with Charles Carter.

Mr Jesse Carter had had no previous experience in the business of tilemaking, and consequently many were the mistakes made in the early days of this firm's existence, the needful experience having to be bought, as usual in such cases, at heavy cost. However, by dint of perseverance all difficulties were overcome, and today the firm probably make as many tiles as any other firm in the country, besides doing a considerable trade in constructional faience and terracotta. . . . The works at East Quay, Poole, are principally occupied in the manufacture of glazed tiles, terracotta, and faience, while those at Hamworthy chiefly produce plain floor-tiles. Messrs Carter have their own clay-beds at Corfe Mullen, where the clay is procured from which their world-famed red tiles are made. Poole is in the centre of the most celebrated clay-fields of the world, and, being a port within easy distance of London and Southampton, it possesses exceptional facilities for shipment of goods to all parts of the world. Messrs. Carter & Co employ a large staff of talented designers and modellers. The utility, variety, and excellence of their products will be readily appreciated by reference to the specimen illustrations they have so kindly permitted to appear in this volume; these, of course, merely represent in a meagre way the fertility of design and product this firm are capable of. To really learn what they can supply, their own illustrated sheets must be studied, or a visit paid to both of their works.

Furnival continued with a report from the Montreal *Daily Witness* of 27 November 1901 which

. . . made some very complimentary comments upon Messrs Carter & Co.'s work in connection with the embellishment of the 'Grand Trunk' general offices. Mr Waite, the architect, they say, desired to produce, not so much a building with a roof on it, as a creation at once useful and beautiful. Today Mr Waite was expressing his satisfaction over the perfect realization, by the firm of Carter & Co., Poole, Dorset, England, of his designs for the vestibule. . . . Then there are panels and friezes for the walls, and the whole work, which occupied Mr Waite for a long time, was sent to the firm mentioned, with the result that modelling, colouring, and general effects are simply, from an art point of view, entrancing. . . . Every piece is perfect; second, that the colouring, which has all to be done by hand, should be so delicate in every piece . . . which comprises the design. The shine of the colour is splendid. Pale yellows and greens – the aesthetic effects will be perfect. This faience will be one of the features of the new offices.[9]

A comment in the Carter & Co. records adds a sobering note to this eulogy. In 1902 an entry details the number of staff working at Carter's who were insured against health risks. The total was 17 and consisted of nine male dippers, dippers' assistants, ware cleaners, glost placers and majolica kiln placers, one male and six female majolica painters and one male glaze grinder and mixer. However, Carter records of lead poisoning are low, for in three years, 1899 – 1901, they note one reported case and one fatality in which lead poisoning was 'doubtful'.[10]

Carter & Co. had expanded enormously by the time Furnival was writing and were to develop further in the next few years. In 1906 a London branch for tile contracting work was established under the control of Arthur Owen Carter (the son of Alfred, Charles' and Owen's elder brother), in the Essex Street offices. In

Figure of a lion advertising Poole production. Carter's also made this lion in an upright, seated position closely based on the *lion séjant* designed by Alfred Stevens (a local man, born in Blandford, Dorset) for the forecourt railings of the British Museum in 1852 and widely copied. *Victoria & Albert Museum.*

1908 Carter & Co. were registered as a joint stock company, limited, with a capital of £75,000.[11]

Bill Eason (Alfred Eason's son) joined the faience department drawing office at East Quay in 1909 and gives an account of the procedure from the first order to the assembly of the finished shop or public house front.

The architect produced preliminary drawings which the head of the department, James Radley Young, would make up into a complete design to an eighth scale with elevations. These would then be sent to the architect with the price. On their return with an agreement, Bill Eason then made detailed half-scale drawings, going to the site with the contractor to assess any problems such as steel supports. Once approval had been gained for these and the increased price – to cover steel supports and any other extras – he would make full-size drawings allowing for one inch in the foot shrinkage. These would then be sent down to the plaster shop.

Construction of this work was divided between parts which were moulded and parts which were made directly in the clay. An area

'Tile decorating', from a Carter & Co. brochure. *c.* 1904. *Photograph: Victoria & Albert Museum.*

of panelling, repeated, would be moulded. The original section was made in plaster and lengths of moulding 'pulled out' with a zinc template taken from the full-size drawing. Bosses or swags set on such back sections were modelled in clay applied to the plaster. The modellers acquired, in addition to their artistic skills, an aptitude for lobbing a ball of clay accurately at the required place on a column front before climbing a gantry to start sculpting. In order to make plaster moulds which could be re-used, the undercut sections of decorative work were filled with plaster slips or wedges so that the mould itself could be lifted straight off the face and the work finished off by hand. Old moulds were broken up and taken over to the Isle of Wight in sailing ketches and used in the man-

The design studio, from a Carter & Co. brochure. *c*. 1904. Left to right: James Radley Young; I. F. Watkins, assistant to Radley Young; Miss Wright, assistant; Edwin Page Turner, at the easel; Miss Jessie Houliston, assistant; Miss Maggie Pearce, assistant. Carter & Co.'s design studio was situated at the east end of the three storey building, East Quay. *Mrs C. J. N. Unwin.*

ufacture of cement. At slack times in the faience works, men were employed in removing irons from the moulds, for re-use.

Some large sections such as scrolls and capitals were made directly in the clay, the scrolling pulled out in the same way, with a template. Once all the clay parts were made they were dried and then fired through the biscuit kiln. After firing the work was set out on the floor where it was fitted – chiselled and filed – and then marked up for glazing. Carter's used, in the main, a range of golden greens and browns, including a rich darker brown. The glaze was floated on, a skilled man being knowledgeable enough to apply the glaze more thickly where it was likely to flow off in the kiln. The work was then glost fired, fitted up again, numbered for assembly (the numbers were painted on the unglazed sides) and despatched. Occasionally the type of fixing meant that screw heads were exposed and so had to be concealed under small ceramic rosettes.[12] In effect, constructional work of this type consisted of a series of faience boxes – made of a rough, high-fired body – which, on assembly, were filled with cement.

In addition to the main work of producing constructional faience, glazed bricks (made by two men operating a hand press), decorative tiles and tile panels, Carter & Co. at East Quay were also making garden wares. Soon after 1900 they were one of the firms contracted to Liberty & Co., in London, for whom they produced balustrading, fountains, pergolas and large pots. The procedure may have been for Liberty's to send them complete working drawings from their own designers such as Archibald Knox. Identifiable pieces that survive are in the traditional Celtic style, decorated with interlaced knots. However, it is known that James Radley Young modelled the prototypes before the moulds were made,[13] and possibly he also made the designs according to Liberty's general specifications. These pots were made in a red terracotta body and Carter's were producing them between 1900–10. They were fired in big muffle kilns, and also in open kilns in which the wares were covered with newspaper plastered with wet clay to prevent them being 'flashed' in the firing. One small surviving pot with Celtic-style decoration is covered with a white tin glaze, an early Radley Young trial in what was to become a major field of glaze experiment at Poole some years later.

Insight into the unsophisticated but nevertheless viable methods of any pottery at this time, still tied to the nineteenth century, is

only available through first-hand accounts and interviews. Bill
Eason provided, for instance, a vivid picture of rows of reddish-
brown Celtic-style pots for Liberty's stored on the roof at Poole
and, leaning against them, frames of architectural designs developing into blue prints in the seaside sunshine.[14]

The workforce at East Quay was augmented at this time (around
1909) by the shutdown of the terracotta department of another
local works, the South-Western Pottery, owned by George Jen-
nings, which had been producing architectural terracotta in red
and also a very good buff-coloured body for many years. Probably

'Working a mosaic pattern', from a Carter & Co. brochure. *c.* 1904. *Photograph:
Victoria & Albert Museum.*

their clay pits ran out at this point, for many of their modellers and finishers came to Carter's.[15]

The chief sculptor working at Carter's was William Carter Unwin (no relation to the Carter family). He was born in Sheffield in 1864, where he studied at the Art School and formed a lifelong friendship with James Radley Young. From there he went as a National Scholar to the National Art Training School in South Kensington, where he completed his studies in 1892 by winning a gold medal for a 'model of a figure from the nude in relief'.[16] During 1893 he went on a travelling scholarship to Italy, France

'Modelling', from a Carter & Co. brochure. *c.* 1904. *Photograph: Victoria & Albert Museum.*

and Belgium. On his return, after a short time at Leicester Art School, he started at Carter's sculpture department in 1896. He worked on all the architectural faience and in particular on figures for public houses – white harts, black dogs, red lions and the like. The figure from the recently demolished White Hart public house in Poole High Street was by him and is now in the local museum. He also trained the future luminary of the faience works, Harry Brown. In about 1919 or 1920 he took up a full-time teaching post in the sculpture department at Bournemouth Art School,[17] having previously taught part-time at Poole Hill Art School and at the Borough School of Art, Poole. On his retirement from Bournemouth on 30 March 1931 'the staff gave him a substantial cheque and a settee in tapestry'.[18] He died in 1935.

In the last years before the First World War developments were beginning which became of major significance after the war. The head of the design department, James Radley Young, emerged as an innovatory artist of the first importance. From accounts – and there are many people who remember him vividly, with respect and affection – he was a man of distinctive personality. His passion was pottery, particularly hand-made, hand-decorated wares. He was especially keen on Spanish and Portuguese styles and used to say that he liked to be able to see and feel that a human being had been involved in the making of a piece. He disliked the practice of turning and buffing down fingermarks and throwing lines, a significant attitude in the light of imminent developments at Poole. He is remembered as a flamboyant dresser in a large, floppy tie, gaiters, velvet jacket, a hat, and a pipe which he is said to have smoked even when riding to work on his bicycle.[19] In about 1901 he married, and shortly before the birth of his first child at the end of that year he left Carter's and went to Haslemere to start a pottery of his own. Here he concentrated on his own lustre glazing and also on incised decoration through cream slip. He had one wood-fired kiln with which he had almost continuous trouble, and the venture was never a success. While at Haslemere he continued to accept commissions for designs and drawings from local builders, hoteliers and breweries with whom he had established a reputation during his nine years at Poole. In effect he was doing the same work as before, but as a freelance, with Carter's making up and fixing the faience which he designed. This source of income was not, however, enough to support his artistic but unprofitable

The 'Brunhild' design, garden pot made by Carter & Co. for Liberty & Co. 1904.
Cecil Higgins Museum.

From 'Garden Pottery', a catalogue illustrating frost-proof earthenware sold by
Liberty & Co. of the type made by Carter & Co. *c.* 1905. *Victoria & Albert Museum.*

THE NEW GARDEN POTTERY IN RED OR GREY FROST PROOF EARTHENWARE
DESIGNED AND MADE BY LIBERTY & CO

LIBERTY & CO   GOLD MEDAL AWARD   LONDON
                       ROYAL BOTANIC SOCIETY OF LONDON   & PARIS

experiments, and after two years he was forced to close down the pottery and to return to Carter's in 1904.[20]

At about the time of Radley Young's return, Edwin Page Turner left the firm. In 1904 he was recorded as receiving £41 12s, a lion's share of that year's profits; his name does not appear again. Radley Young was left in charge not only of the design department and of all architectural faience, but also of the decorative and painted scenic tile panels. Radley Young's work in this department had fostered Carter's reputation as one of the foremost British tile-works. They had kept abreast of current trends, under his and Owen's influence, moving into *Art Nouveau* painted patterns on lustre-glazed tiles and into the production of vases and other pottery in the same style. Until the outbreak of the First World War, however, they had never been seen to be ahead of, or independent of the general commercial movement.

3

1914-1920

War-time production, early painted pots and the Omega Workshops

W I T H the outbreak of war the fortunes of the potteries were brought to crisis point, and Owen Carter and James Radley Young were forced to devise new ways of employing the much reduced workforce. In 1913 the first Dressler continuous gas-fired tunnel kiln had been installed at the White Works, Hamworthy, for firing white- and cream-glazed tiles. Carter & Co. were the second tile-works in England to install a Dressler kiln, after J. H. Barrett & Co. Ltd[1] at Stoke-on-Trent. The following year D.O.R.A. (the Defence of the Realm Act) came into force, with its limits on the production of any but the most essential building materials, including decorative tiles. In their search for alternative production, Carter's made commemorative wares such as portrait plaques of war-time leaders. Several are known and they include a large (8¼ in. × 8¼ in.) portrait of Gladstone, which indicates that this was not a new venture for Carter's. Of the war-time ones three are known, the first two of Lord Kitchener and Lord Jellicoe. These were modelled from photographs, presumably by someone such as W. C. Unwin in the faience modelling shop. Unwin is known to have made a portrait bust of James Radley Young and of Thomas Hardy, after several sittings with the writer,[2] and was a skilled portraitist. The Kitchener plaque was based on a photograph by the society photographer, Bassano, while the source for Lord Jellicoe's portrait was an official photograph of him in captain's uniform, taken immediately after the Boxer Rebellion in 1901. Local dignitaries were also recorded in this way; van Raalte, Mayor of Poole at the time, is the third example. The modelled surfaces of the plaques were covered with a clear coloured glaze

Sheet showing various patterns in marble mosaic, from a Carter & Co. catalogue.
c. 1917. *Victoria & Albert Museum.*

Sheet showing encaustic and plain tiles, from a Carter & Co. catalogue.
c. 1917. *Victoria & Albert Museum.*

Plaque, with a modelled portrait of Lord Kitchener from a
photograph by the society photographer, Bassano. Dated 1914.
Victoria & Albert Museum.

which settled more thickly into the recessed areas and gave the image an uncannily accurate likeness to the photographic portraits. This was an established technique used by several other tile manufacturers in Britain, Europe and America, such as George Cartlidge at Adams and Cartlidge, Wedgwood, Sherwin and Cotton and also the Cambridge Art Tile Works, Kentucky.

Owen Carter experimented with the production of beads on which he continued to use his lustre glazes, in reds and blues. These are said to have been produced not only for the local market, where apparently they sold very well, but also for export.[3] Accounts exist in which Owen is said to have designed a specially small kiln in which to fire the beads.[4] In addition Carter's made perforated 'perfume bricks' of an absorbent, unglazed body which were filled with a scented oil, and also firelighters on the same principle.[5] Even laboratory wares, in a porcellaneous body, are believed to have been made.[6] Such experiments kept some of the kilns and the remaining employees occupied, although throughout the war years problems were caused by inferior coal and the impossibility of obtaining spare parts or of making repairs.

These projects formed the major part of the activities at Poole and Hamworthy, but at the same time more significant events were afoot. Early in the war Radley Young (J.R.Y. as he became known to those who worked under him) apparently re-discovered his earlier ambitions in the pottery field, saw his opportunity and grasped it. He formed a new pottery unit, taking girls from the decorating and modelling shops where they had been employed in painting decorative designs on tiles, throwing and, in the case of Lily Gilham who was especially talented, in modelling figures of insects and reptiles, and applying them to vases and other shapes. Lily Gilham moved from modelling to trailing slip outline decoration in the tile shops and finally to the pottery unit where she learnt, under J.R.Y, to become a highly skilful thrower. Individualism was encouraged and she became proficient at making thin, fine wares, each piece a little different from the last. Beginning with only two girls who were gradually joined by others, the new unit was to start producing domestic pottery of a type not seen before at Poole, and some of it completely innovatory. They began by making an unglazed ware and then two types of glazed wares, one painted with small flower sprigs, the other with simple patterns of blue lines which became known as Blue Stripe Ware.

The unglazed ware, which was the first of these new developments, was a very radical move and there seems to be no immediate precedent for it. It has been suggested that the source was the collection of Roman pots excavated in the area and housed in the local museums.[7] This is very probable, and certainly there are close links in the treatment of the body, the absence of glazes and particularly in the shapes which, during the early years, consisted mainly of lipped bowls, simple dishes and funnel-shaped vases. Occasionally a smear glaze was applied to the bowls to counteract porosity. The painted decoration in shades of brown was limited to simple zig-zags and loops, again reminiscent of primitive pattern-making, although in this the Poole designers may have been conscious of the fashionable, contemporary interest in pre-Columbian and African decoration. The body was the fairly coarse grey-white clay used in tile production, and the earliest surviving examples are very crudely made and the patterns inexpertly painted. Nevertheless even these examples (in the Victoria and Albert Museum and Poole Pottery Ltd collections) are impressed with the Carter & Co. signature, indicating that the Pottery began selling them very early. Carter & Co. are recorded in the catalogue of the British Industries Fair of 1917 as contributing to the Art Pottery section.

The other two types heralded the later production of floral decorated pottery which became Poole's most distinctive ware. At this time J.R.Y. had a specialist glaze maker working with him, probably Alfred Eason, the man who had collaborated with Owen Carter on the lustres and who was by this time works manager.[8] Just before the war Eason and Young developed and reintroduced the soft tin glazes which they called 'Delft'. The two new lines were made in the same grey-white body used for the lustred vases. Also, for the first time and possibly as early as 1915,[9] the red or salmon-coloured clay, previously only used in the tile and garden ware production, was introduced into the pottery works. The method began by coating the biscuit-fired piece with a grey-white slip. The undecorated interior was then covered with partially opaque glaze and the exterior, which was to be decorated, with a clear glaze. The painting was applied before firing and very often in soluble colours, which accounts for the attractive, soft, slightly fuzzy appearance, although in this earliest production the blue was usually the only colour which was soluble in this way. A long-standing rumour says that this technique was brought over to Poole during the war by Belgian refugees. The only Belgian so far discovered to be connected with Carter's is Joseph Roelants, who made designs for the Tileworks. He arrived in England in about 1914 with his wife and two children, probably from Antwerp. He was a trained potter and certainly was involved with the first production in the Delft technique at Poole.[10] It is possible that he and other un-named refugees, absorbed into the Carter workforce during the war at this time of experiment, may by their presence have sown the idea of using the Delft technique of in-glaze painted decoration. However, the method was used in the nineteenth century by other potteries, such as Minton where Alfred Eason had worked. Consequently the technique was known, had recently been in use in Britain, and experiments may already have been under way.

The decoration devised for these two painted lines was simple in the extreme, well within the capabilities of trainee paintresses. The skill with which these earliest pots were painted varies considerably, as with the unglazed ware. Some of the girls were already experienced in painting decoration, having worked in the tile decorating shops, while others were new to the work. The Blue Stripe patterns range from plain stripes from top to bottom, with possibly a plain stripe around the rim, to rather more elaborate versions including diamonds and lozenges. The flower sprigs at this stage are no more than a two- or three-colour motif of petals, a stalk and a few leaves.

Simultaneously with the production of these wares at Poole, an enterprise based in London resulted in an influx of people and ideas which connect Poole with one of the most important British art movements of the period.

In 1913 the art critic Roger Fry began the Omega Workshops. The logical outcome from his support of young English artists was to develop a scheme in which they might both practise their art and enjoy some form of paid employment. He saw the artists engaged in 'some craft in which his artistic powers would be constantly occupied, although at a lower tension and in a humbler way'.[11] Fry's particular battle was against a philistine establishment and an apathetic public, antagonistic and indifferent to the continental developments in art, especially in France. Coincidentally, the year in which he launched the Omega also saw the first interest and appreciation by the public in an exhibition of Post-Impressionist painting – the second show of this work which Fry arranged. This interest encouraged him to hope that England might at last prove receptive to the work of young painters such as Duncan Grant, Vanessa Bell, Wyndham Lewis and Augustus John. For some time he had been established as the champion of this generation of artists. Public appreciation of French art, however, did not immediately alter the existing circumstances under which the English painters struggled, and so a small legacy and the irresistible logic of the Workshop idea meant that at the age of forty-six he plunged into organizing, launching and selling the new scheme.

The young artists were to be paid thirty shillings a week and were to make not only pottery, but furniture, printed and decorated textiles, embroideries, dresses and carpets. Much of the design work also came from Fry, as well as the administrative and commercial responsibilities. In the preface of the advertising booklet he produced, he clearly stated his aims.

The Omega Workshops Limited is a group of artists who are working with the object of allowing free play to the delight in creation in the making of objects for common life. They refuse to spoil the expressive quality of their work by sandpapering it down to a shop finish, in the belief that the public has at last seen through the humbug of the machine-made imitation of works of art. They endeavour to satisfy practical necessities in a workmanlike manner, but not to flatter by the pretentious elegance of the machine-made article. They try to keep the spontaneous freshness of primitive or peasant work, while satisfying the needs and expressing the feelings of the modern cultivated man.

His thoughts on the production of pottery, specifically, are set down.

. . . of all crafts none has suffered more than pottery from the application of scientific commercialism. We now use almost entirely articles which have lost all direct expressiveness of surface modelling. Our cups and saucers are reduced by machine turning to a dead mechanical exactitude and uniformity. Pottery is essentially a form of sculpture, and its surface should express directly the artist's sensibility both of proportion and surface. The Omega pottery is made on the wheel by artists and is not merely executed to their design. It therefore represents, as scarcely any modern pottery does, this expressive character. It is made for the most part with a white tin glaze analogous to that of old Delft.

The advertised range of Omega pottery was 'Ashtrays, Inkstands, letter-weights, etc., from 3/- to 5/-. Jam Pots, Cruet Stands, Salad Bowls, etc. Tiles for Fireplaces painted to order. Handpainted Tea Sets to order at moderate prices. Vases and Bowls suitable for flowers, Large Jars, Jugs, etc.'[12]

This booklet was published in about 1915 when the Omega was in full swing, but in 1913 there were many preliminary difficulties to overcome. Fry's earliest pottery productions were of commercially-made pieces decorated by Duncan Grant and others. Obviously this denied Fry's basic principles, and shortly after, still in 1913, he began visiting an un-named pottery in Mitcham, Surrey. The potter there was given designs to work from and in addition Fry began taking lessons in throwing his own shapes. He was accompanied by Vanessa Bell, but while he achieved some success in throwing to a standard regularly, she was primarily a decorator. Their efforts brought some acclaim from a representative from the British Museum who admired the wares and in particular a turquoise glaze, which Fry thought probably an unrepeatable accident in the firing.

In 1914 the Mitcham potter joined the army and Fry had to find some alternative pottery at which to carry on his work. His secretary and friend Miss Winifred Gill recommended Carter and Co. at Poole. Fry's enthusiasm for the soft, warm, white tin glaze, the blacks, blues and yellows, would have found no more receptive pottery than that at East Quay, where glaze experiments and new colours were being enthusiastically developed under Owen and J.R.Y. with Alfred Eason. Very probably the fact that both Fry and many of the Carter family were Quakers was an added attraction. It was arranged that Roger, Charles Carter's son, should come up to London to meet Fry at the Omega. The Workshop had been a social success almost instantly and Fry spent a great deal of his time showing potential customers and amused society people around the showrooms in Fitzroy Square. Real selling was hard work, but orders began to come in from both England and abroad and that hallmark of success, the problem of copyists, troubled him very early on. In 1914 the war-struck pottery took the opportunity to begin production of a selling line. Miss Gill tells of an amusing exchange during that interview between Roger Carter and Fry.

F R Y: 'The first question I want to ask you is, "What is your body like?" '

C A R T E R: 'Hard, pretty hard, and I think I can promise you it is watertight.'[13]

Fry and Carter were happy with the arrangement and so Fry began travelling down to Poole where he continued to learn the arts of throwing, glazing and decorating. According to his biographer, Virginia Woolf, the lodgings at Poole were squalid and the classical ladies' heads on the cast-iron fireplace so unbearable that Fry was compelled to obliterate them with clay. However, he spent long hours at the Pottery and amazingly, despite the war, by 1916 orders were coming in from Norway, Sweden and California. The pressure of work on him increased as artists were called up, although, according to Virginia Woolf, one conscientious objector was employed by the Omega.[14] Unaided, he struggled, discovering for himself the simple and traditional ribbon handle.[15] In 1915, while still supporting the Omega, Fry was working with his sisters to organize the Quaker Relief Fund in France and by this time too, Roger Carter and his twin brother Harry had equipped an ambulance and gone across to France to help with the wounded.[16]

Unfortunately there is no record of James Radley Young's opinions of the Fry productions, although, given his known predilection for peasant and traditional pottery, he must have been interested and sympathetic. However, despite the absence of documentation, there is a group of wares which hold a particular interest. These are owned by Poole Pottery Ltd and have been at the works since their production in about 1915–16. The most interesting are a ewer and basin, *en suite*, freely painted in blues and yellows on white tin glaze, with bands of foliate panels interspaced with horizontal lines, circles and crosses. The style of painting closely matches that of Vanessa Bell, Duncan Grant and James Radley Young, leaving little doubt that the professional and competent artist must have been one of these three. The pieces are impressed 'Carter & Co.' in script, incised '8' (the basin), and '9' (the ewer) and noted in pencil 'No 34' (the basin) and 'No 33 50/-

Vase with a lustrous green glaze. Dated 1908. *Victoria & Albert Museum.*

Ewer & Basin' (the ewer), indicating that these were Carter production shapes, possibly exhibited. The first part of the introduction to the Omega booklet illuminates the background against which these pieces were made:

If you look at a pot or a woven cloth by a negro savage of the Congo with the crude instruments at his disposal, you may begin despising it for its want of finish. If you put them beside a piece of modern Sèvres china or a velvet brocade from a Lyons factory, you will perhaps begin by congratulating yourself upon the wonders of modern industrial civilisation, and think with pity of the poor savage. But if you allow the poor savage's handiwork a longer contemplation you will find something in it of greater value and significance than in the Sèvres china or Lyons velvet.

It will become apparent that the negro enjoyed making his pot or cloth, that he pondered delightedly over the possibilities of his craft and that his enjoyment finds expression in many ways; and as these become increasingly apparent to you, you share his joy in creation, and in that forget the roughness of the result. On the other hand the modern factory products were made almost entirely for gain, no other joy than that of money entered into their creation. You may admire the skill which has been revealed in this, but it can communicate no disinterested delight.

The artist is the man who creates not only for need but for joy, and in the long run mankind will not be content without sharing that joy through the possession of real works of art, however humble or unpretentious they may be.[17]

This philosophy was apparently shared by James Radley Young and the ewer and basin, well made and painted, are consequently of special interest. The skill with which they have been thrown make it certain that they were made by Radley Young or one of the Pottery's throwers, such as Lily Gilham, while the spirit behind the decoration is that of the creative artist in the fine art tradition.

The Omega wares, however, were crude by most standards. The pieces are heavy, the result of less than expert throwing. Where usual production methods would have fined down the excess of clay and irregular shapes, Fry's basic dictum not only prevented this but lauded the results of his unskilled efforts, although, according to Miss Gill, he did use the Pottery to the extent of having his original pieces 'jollied' where possible, so that they could be produced in numbers. They are interesting, and certainly the shapes were novel and an important contribution to the Omega aims.

Fry's concept was linked to a fine art basis. The Omega productions were seen by him as art rather than design and this is the claim he made in the preface to the advertising booklet already quoted. The Continental 'Modern Movement' meant to him the exciting post-Cézanne developments in French painting rather than the industrial design innovations in Germany. However, in a long term view the shapes he developed undoubtedly foreshadow ceramic design of the late 1920s. While he suffered from copyists in the textile and furniture fields, it was not until ten or twelve years later that the ceramic industry moved away from the *Art Nouveau* style and began to make significant strides towards a truly

Left: unglazed vase painted in dark brown. *c.* 1914–18.
Poole Pottery Ltd. Right: vase, glazed inside, painted in
black and brown. 1925–30. *Victoria & Albert Museum.*
Both vases designed by James Radley Young.

modern twentieth-century style. In the mid-to-late 1920s ceramic
design in England began to take on a more angular, cleaner line
and shapes became more positive, in the Fry manner. However,
instead of the Omega the influential factor was the International
Exhibition held in Paris in 1925, and the resultant awareness was
not only of French design but also of Scandinavian and German
developments. Even Carter's, who had more opportunity than
most, did not benefit from close contact with Fry's forward-looking,
if unpolished, ideas on tureens and teapots. It was the painted
decoration that had most influence and in which the firm excelled
in its formative years. In 1916 opinion among the Pottery employees, understandably, was confined to amusement and the view that
to be 'modern' one had only to produce convex rather than concave
saucers, so the visiting artists were undoubtedly *avant-garde*. Prob-

ably it was this very lack of skill and professionalism in the making that prevented the commercial firms from seeing any virtue in the wares, if they considered them at all. In this they missed the stylish simplicity, the use of plain, undecorated glazes in strong colours – the white tin, black, blue, yellow and purple – and some very striking painted designs, both geometric or abstract patterns and figurative designs, by Duncan Grant and Vanessa Bell. Another contributor to Omega production was the potter Phyllis Keyes, who specialized in casting wares, and the two painters continued after the demise of the Workshops to collaborate with her, decorating wares through the 1920s and into the 1930s.

The only other potteries which benefited from Fry's activities were Brain & Co., under Thomas Acland Fennemore, and A. J. Wilkinson & Co., under Clarice Cliff, who experimented with a range of artist-decorated tableware in 1932–3. Two of the artists commissioned were Duncan Grant and Vanessa Bell and they produced several attractive and colourful designs which were first shown in an exhibition at Harrod's in 1934.

In June 1919 the Omega closed down with a sale of the remaining stock. During the last year of the war production and selling had become an overwhelming burden, and a year later Fry decided to give up the unequal struggle. A last note in Virginia Woolf's biography describes Fry's own home in the 1920s: 'On the dinner table, decorated by Duncan Grant, were the plates he had made with his own hands, and round it were the chairs he had designed himself'.[18] He visited the Pottery at Poole briefly in the mid–1920s[19] but by then his energies were once more directed towards lecturing and painting.

Carter's own production had slowed down almost to a standstill by 1918. Virtually no pottery was made, and very few tiles. In 1917 Radley Young was recruited into war work, which meant he was transferred across to the new shipyard at Hamworthy which had been built to construct barges. There his skills as a draughtsman were employed in making drawings for the shipyard workshops. He spent about eighteen months there, until the Armistice.[20]

On his return to Poole he was involved in the post-war labour troubles which sprang up at Carter's. Men coming back from the forces to the works were offered wages still set at near pre-war levels. The drawing office staff were paid £2, for instance, with no overtime payment despite working as much as sixty or seventy hours a week on occasions. Approaches were made through the company secretary, Ben Elford, and eventually their pay was increased.[21] James Radley Young made recommendations on behalf of his staff, and consequently was identified with these grievances.[22] This position, combined with the inevitable clean sweep of pre-war associations, resulted in his being overlooked at the time of the re-organization of the company and the setting-up of a new directorship. He never regained his former prominence and favoured status. Curiously, his name does not appear on the records of profit-sharing after 1900. His brief attempt to set up independently towards the end of 1901 may have cost him any extra financial rewards after his return. In 1919 the death of Owen, with whom he had worked so closely, left him without any support from the one influential person to whom he might have appealed at this critical point. However, it was a time of great change and with the new decade Carter & Co. began a new life.

In 1920 a report was issued 'to those who work with Carter & Co. Ltd., Poole', written by Cyril Carter, Charles' son,[23] which summed up the position two years after the end of the war. The situation was very much in the balance. While the tile-making side was picking up, despite desperate difficulties with kilns and equip-ment, the pottery side was still underdeveloped and, although surprising successes had been achieved for such a new venture, its future was by no means certain. The report makes the conditions quite clear.

What, then, have we been able to do so far?

Take P O O L E first. A friend who knew the works well eighteen months ago, visiting it recently, said he could hardly find his way about.

Poole was our first works and is our worst works: it grew as the business grew, and it grew just as things were needed, without any preconceived plan as to the whole. It would be better for all of us if we could build a new works at Hamworthy, where we have plenty of room to do it, for the work that we now do at Poole.

In the early part of last year we were still making our faience at Poole and firing most of it at the White Works, through the Dressler. We could not get suitable coal for enamel kilns at Poole. This was not an efficient nor economical way of doing things. Then, in the autumn of 1919 we were offered two large ceramic marble jobs, which we took, perhaps rather against our better judgment. We had not the facilities for doing two large jobs at Poole, and had to discuss the possibility of building

Bottle, painted in purple and greens, designed by
James Radley Young. *c.* 1917–20. *Victoria & Albert
Museum.*

workshops and a ceramic marble kiln at Hamworthy. On consideration
however, we came to the conclusion that we could quickly make sufficient
alterations to the Poole Works, and put in a certain amount of new plant,
which would enable us to carry out these jobs and manufacture fairly
efficiently for the time being; also that the large cost involved in new
buildings at Hamworthy would not be justified. But plant for the new
drying stove, promised by the engineers to be running by the middle of
January, was not in use until April!

We went straight on with a new ceramic marble kiln – which was first
fired at the end of March 1920. We have pulled down two large round
kilns, which were no longer wanted, and enlarged and improved the
making shops.

We converted several old buildings and removed the handcraft pottery
into them, thus making it a separate department by itself, and releasing
valuable space required by the faience department.

We made a large floor for laying out ceramic marble in the space where
a round kiln stood, and we shall utilize the heat from the ceramic marble
kilns (another is now being built, making three with the original small

one) for drying clay. As a temporary measure a fan was installed to work the ceramic marble kiln, but this will be augmented by a shaft as soon as the bricklayers are available, the fan possibly being used when the kilns are in full fire.

We have made a new blowing shop which was intended for ceramic marble but has been used for an experiment in one-fire faience, and will probably be used shortly for the purpose for which it was originally prepared. This shop is conveniently near the stove and ceramic marble kilns.

A good deal of work has been done in the heating of the workshops.

Those of you who know Poole Works will understand that it has been difficult, with badly arranged and often badly built old buildings, to evolve an efficient works. It would be very much easier to start afresh. One thing we have been trying to do is to get some mechanical system of carrying heavy articles like moulds, large blocks of faience and terra-cotta, from the maker to the stoves and thence to the kilns, and for carrying clay, etc., to the makers. Any such system is necessarily expensive, and is rendered more so in our case by the awkward way in which buildings are placed, and the fact that floor levels vary so much. We decided that one system, which was suggested to us by an experienced consulting engineer, whose opinion we took and who prepared a scheme, would not be justified in view of the cost involved. It is still possible that we may be able to do something in this direction.

One thing we have done is to put in electric light all over the works. We shall probably take this from the local supply shortly, and use electricity to run what little machinery is necessary at night.

We have now before us, and are considering, plans for new lavatory and sanitary accommodation, and when this is done – and the scheme includes a new mess-room and rest-room for girls – we do not think anything we can do, short of rebuilding the whole place, would materially improve the Poole Works.

At the A.P. things were better. The speed with which we were able to get going again was largely governed by the way in which demobilized men came back. Perfume bricks kept a little staff busy; large orders for plastic briquettes and tiles for margarine factories only waited for men to make them and coal to burn them. As before the war, we still went on making as much ceramic marble as the one kiln would take, and ordinary floor-tile orders were only waiting to be made, burnt, and sent away. Difficulties there were, of course. For instance, it was sometime before we were able to get the slip-house working for vitreous. Drying accommodation for the plastic department, too, was deficient.

Well, what have we done at the A.P? Very little in the way of plant and buildings. The only new building we have put up is an addition to the packing-shed in which to store packed tiles awaiting shipment for abroad.

We have put in a new mill and sieve for red dust, and have replaced an obsolete set of edge-runners, all of which – mill, sieve, and edge-runners – are of greater capacity than those we had previously. When we can decide on the best position for it we shall also install a machine for sifting and grading grog.

A small experimental tunnel kiln, designed by the late Mr. Owen Carter and Mr. W. Wilkins, and built by the latter, has been completed and tried. The idea has proved a complete success, and with certain adaptations may prove to be a very important improvement on other methods of firing. Great credit is due to W. Wilkins for the way in which he has carried his idea – for he is very largely responsible for it – to a successful conclusion.

As to things we have to do here and are now considering: better drying facilities for pugged clay and the plastic-made goods, the heating of the press rooms and workshops in the winter, and above all, as at Poole, the provision of lavatory and sanitary accommodation for men and women. This latter is somewhat dependent on whether the public sewerage scheme for Hamworthy is proceeded with. The possibility and advisability of making bricks to use up the large quantities of waste clays that we are bound to accumulate is also being considered.

We had under consideration for a long time, and decided upon, a scheme for a light railway to link up the A.P. with the White Works; but although certain of the material was bought and delivered, difficulties with engineers who were dealing with the matter have caused it to be abandoned for the time being, to give way to more urgent matters. And although this has been under consideration since the summer of last year, the Poole Town Council have not yet given the necessary sanction to cross the road between the two works.

We still think that considerable benefit and economy of working would be derived from some such scheme, and hope to put it into operation if the outlay appears to be justified.

The WHITE WORKS position at the end of the war was rather different. Here, when it reigns at all, the Dressler Oven reigns supreme. The Dressler is fickle but autocratic. When it condescends to work at all, it must be fed; and fed it was, with such white-glazed and enamels as we were able to make, with fireplace work, with faience, with beads, and perfume bricks.

Now the faience is fired at Poole, where it is made. Perfume bricks and beads, having fulfilled a useful purpose, form a decreasing portion of the Dressler menu. Fireplace work is nearly all done at Poole. And the Dressler calls for tiles, tiles, tiles!

Two-handled jar and cover, decorated in blue and
yellow. Probably designed by James Radley Young,
showing the influence of Vanessa Bell. 1914–20. *Victoria
& Albert Museum.*

We have said that the Dressler is fickle. We had almost said something
stronger – much stronger. It is almost like the little girl who, 'when she
was good was very good indeed, but when she was bad she was . . .' the
very devil. During the last eighteen months we have struggled and struggled, always hoping almost against hope. No patient has ever been more
tenderly nursed. At last it was decided that a serious operation was
necessary. She was given practically a new inside, the producer was
rebuilt on lines approved by recent experience and everything looked rosy
again. 'At last', we thought, 'we shall be able to get away all these orders
that have been waiting for so many months; we shall be able to please all
those customers to whom we have had to say, "a little patience, you shall
have your tiles next week" ' – that next week which like tomorrow, never
comes. Well, our hopes have been partly realized. The sickly invalid,
turning out a paltry 700 yards a week and sometimes less, is now giving
us something like 1,800 yards a week, and when we have made certain

other alterations as to loading of trucks, will give us considerably more. But, as if we had not had enough trouble, enter, as in a melodrama, the demon 'blue-edge'. Those of you whose work has taken you anywhere near the tunnel will know this only too well. It is now not so much the question, 'How is the Dressler this morning?' as 'How is the "blue-edge"?' that is heard on all hands. However, we think now – and the most experienced tile-makers in the country were unable to tell us to what the trouble was due – that we look like laying this ghost.

Donald Farmer says that the problem arose during the storing of the glazed tiles before glost firing. The glaze was sprayed on to the tiles (the sprayer was powered by a man operating a pump), and in order to spray finely and evenly enough a certain amount of gelatine was mixed in with the glaze. While tiles were stacked awaiting the final firing, the edges dried out and the gelatine was lost to some extent. In the kiln, while the still damp centres fired satisfactorily, the edges carbonized and this became known as the 'blue-edge'. The report continues:

Much of our trouble with the Dressler has been due to the poor quality of coke we have been able to obtain. We have, therefore, in common with other possessors of Dressler ovens, to use a small proportion of coal with the coke. But only certain coals will do, and these have at times been difficult or impossible to get.

There is practically no limit to the number of white glazed tiles that is wanted in this country and abroad. The difficulty is to turn them out fast enough.

It is easy enough to be wise after the event, but we should have been wiser, when the Dressler first began to give serious trouble, to have overhauled it thoroughly then; but, with customers clamouring for goods, we were always hoping against hope that it would be 'better in the morning'.

The White Works centres round and is governed by the Dressler. But we have had other problems. Now that the Dressler is producing more, and is likely to produce more still, we must make more tiles. Owing partly to certain altered conditions we were able to make, the press-room has recently increased its output by 20%. If all the tiles made in the press-room went through the kilns and eventually reached the dipping shops as good biscuit, all would be well. But only 90 of every 100 are good enough to be dipped.

Then, with the press-room making more tiles we must have more dust; that means dry clay, which means more flint, more raw materials.

We have bought and installed a more modern type of filter press for

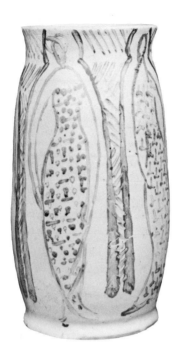

Vase, almost certainly made by Roger Fry and
decorated by Vanessa Bell in blue and yellow, for the
Omega Workshops Ltd. 1914–18. *Victoria & Albert
Museum.*

clay which was not very satisfactory at first but is now doing well, owing
to a suggestion made by the man in charge of it.

The clay drying problem is one which we have to tackle. We have
made a quite inefficient arrangement as a temporary measure, and are
now making what we hope will be a further improvement, but the whole
question of efficient clay drying must be dealt with.

To deal with the increased output which we are getting and which we
want – which the country wants – we shall probably have to build a new
biscuit-oven.

As to the other works, plant and building want attention and repair,
but pressure of work has only enabled us to do patching so far.

A new packing shed is urgently wanted and is being built. The roofs
at all three works are being made watertight.

We do not want to talk too much about our troubles, but it is not a
bad thing that you should realize that things are not always as easy as
they seem. A man or woman, working at his or her own job, often sees
ways in which things might be done better, perhaps makes a suggestion
for improvement, and may be disappointed that the suggestion is not
immediately acted upon. We want that man or woman to realize that,
important as his or her suggestion may be, it is probably only one of

many other problems which we have to tackle. There are three separate works and each works has many departments. (Eighteen suggestions have been made by employees for which awards have been made. Seven of these suggestions have been acted on so far.)

Do you know where our tiles go all the year round? We are going to try and show you by putting up photographs of work we have done in different places from time to time.

During the last year we have been more than fully occupied with home trade, but have sent tiles to Canada, South America, India, and China.

We have just completed a large contract for ceramic marble for a music-hall in the North of London, and for a large cinema at Kingston-on-Thames; also a smaller one at Wandsworth.

We can, we think, say without boasting that our Ceramic Marble is the best material of its kind that is made in this country.

We have been very busy with faience work, mostly for public houses.

This is a business which we think we can always get orders for *as long as we keep up the pre-war standard*. It is troublesome stuff to make, and needs the greatest of care from the drawing office to the job – care in making, care in handling. If it is not well made, if mistakes are made in details or in making, causing delays to jobs, it will get a bad name and architects will cease to use it. There is nothing mechanical about faience or terra-cotta making. It is a job for a craftsman, and its quality will depend on the skill with which it is made.

Then many of you know that we supply and fix the wall and floor tiling to Lipton's new shops, for the International Tea Stores, for Peark's Stores. These firms have had to go to other people for some of their tiling recently, owing to the fact that we have not been able to supply fast enough. The architect for one of them was at the works recently and told us that they have sixteen new shops in hand.

So you see there ought to be plenty of work to do if we can only turn out good stuff and do it quickly. And carelessness on the part of one man, resulting in a damaged piece of faience, tiles glazed the wrong colour, and things of that sort, will often hang up a job for weeks.

We have supplied and fixed the 1,000 yards of tiles for the Ebbw Vale Iron Works at their new offices and power houses in South Wales; 2,700 yards at Caley's chocolate factory at Norwich; 600 yards for the Metropolitan Water Board; 1,400 yards for the Glory Mills, High Wycombe.

There is work to be done and we can do it.[24]

4
1921-1930

Carter, Stabler & Adams:
painted wares

T O W A R D S the end of *A Report for the Year 1920* was a brief mention of pot production as it had developed by that year, with various recommendations by contemporary journals.

One word as to our POTS. We are proud of our pots. Started by Mr. Young when things were slack during the war, they have met with a very encouraging reception by the discriminating public, with the result that what started more or less as an experiment has now become an established, though comparatively small, factor in our business, and Carter Pots are to be found all over England, and have spread to America. This has not been done without a lot of very hard work and careful thought on the part of those responsible, to whom great credit is due.

Here is what other people think of our pots.

THE BRITISH CLAYWORKER, JULY 15th, 1920. – 'One of the most promising and successful exhibits in the institute is the work of Messrs. Carter of Poole. This firm has an original display of domestic pottery, apparently made out of a hard-fired terra-cotta body, covered with a durable and most opaque glaze, which not only harmonizes with decorative treatment, but partly shows the body qualities of the ware. The glaze employed has a tendency to craze which if re-adjusted would help to introduce a new and serviceable domestic ware. An improvement by way of better throwing and making in this ware is well worth attention. The institute is doing valuable work in bringing this pottery innovation before the public. Their ceramic marble glaze is an excellent architectural material, and perhaps the fact of it not being too dense in quality may appeal to the taste of certain architects.'

JOURNAL OF THE ROYAL SOCIETY OF ARTS, JUNE 11th, 1920. – 'The simple ware manufactured with skill and taste by Carter, of Poole . . .

introduces to the public ceramics of good design, colour, and workmanship within the reach of all.'

THE HARDWARE TRADE JOURNAL, AUGUST 27th, 1920. – 'In originality
of decoration and good shapes the well-known tile firm of Carter & Co.
Ltd., Poole, have reached a high standard in their hand-thrown, glazed
and unglazed vases, candlesticks, etc. The fresh colours and striking
pattern made up of spots and brushwork stripe effects are in harmony
with the shape; new treatments are green and black, soft mauve and
green, and renderings of Portuguese, Persian, and Moorish styles; also
producing one-piece egg-cups on a flat stand.'[1]

'Picardy Peasants', with blue, white and brown glazes, designed by Phoebe Stabler
in 1911 and made by Carter, Stabler & Adams Ltd. 1921–4. *Poole Pottery Ltd.*
Photograph: Victoria & Albert Museum.

'The Lavender Woman', with purple, blue and buff glazes, designed by Phoebe
Stabler in 1913, made by Carter, Stabler & Adams Ltd and sold by them
throughout the 1920s and early 1930s. *Victoria & Albert Museum.*

'Fighting Cock', with streaked brown glazes, designed by Harold Stabler. 1921–4.
Victoria & Albert Museum.

Cyril Carter had begun to take a driving interest in the fortunes
of the works, particularly in the pottery production. For some years
before 1914 he had worked under his cousin Arthur Owen Carter
(son of Alfred Carter), who managed the London office, which by
1911 moved from Essex Street to 29, Albert Embankment. As part
of this arrangement Cyril worked as a representative selling wares
and acquiring contracts.[2] It was mainly through the contacts he
established at this time and after the war with individuals and
various organizations devoted to the furtherance of good industrial

design that the pottery production began to occupy a position of importance and influence. In about 1920 or 1921 Cyril relinquished his responsibility for the floor tile works (the A.P.) to his brother Roger, and from then on he concentrated on the pottery side.[3]

Towards the end of the war, while he was still in Egypt, Cyril Carter received a letter from his father Charles, telling him that he had just met a man called Harold Stabler with whom he was very impressed. He hoped that Stabler would work with the Pottery in some way and looked forward to hearing Cyril's opinion of him.[4] Presumably Owen's health was already failing, as consultation with him was not mentioned. In 1921, two years after Owen's death, Charles took the decision to set the pottery production on a positive and commercial footing. The new company of Carter, Stabler & Adams was formed.

Harold Stabler had been established for some time as a brilliant designer in gold and silver. His talents extended to enamelling, wood- and stone-carving and graphic design, and he was also an influential teacher at the Royal College of Art and the Sir John Cass Technical Institute. In addition, with his wife Phoebe, he had modelled a number of figures. The Stablers had their own kiln at their home in The Mall, Hammersmith, and their early figures bear their personal backstamp designed around the Hammersmith Bridge motif. Phoebe seems to have been a shrewd businesswoman for she sold to Royal Doulton the reproduction rights of a figure which they first produced in 1913, entitled 'The Madonna of the Square'. Virtually this same figure was also cast and produced in quantity at Poole throughout the 1920s under the name 'The Lavender Woman'. The earliest casts bear the Stablers' backstamp only. In 1911 she also sold the rights of 'The Picardy Peasant' figures to Doulton, which they began producing in 1913 and continued to make until 1938, selling them in competition with the Poole casts under the same title. These were only two of the many Phoebe Stabler designs produced by both Poole and Doulton, while other figures were made by the Ashtead Pottery and, in the 1930s, by Worcester.

Harold Stabler was a founder member of the British Institute of Industrial Art and, more importantly, was on the first council of the Design and Industries Association in 1915, the year in which it was founded. Other members of the council included W. B. Dalton, the potter and principal of the Camberwell School of Arts

Vase, Blue Stripe ware, designed by
James Radley Young and painted by
Ruth Pavely. *c.* 1922. *Private collection.*

Vase, painted in purple, green and blue
by Anne Hatchard, with Grape pattern,
a design by Erna Manners. 1921. *Victoria
& Albert Museum.*

and Crafts; C. H. St. John Hornby of W. H. Smith and Son; Frank
Pick of the Underground Railways; and Ambrose Heal of Heal
and Son, all of whom were to be connected in some way with the
new firm over the next two decades. The rank and file membership
in the inaugural year also included significant and influential
names – Gordon Forsyth, designer, teacher and lecturer; Minnie
McLeish, the textile and poster designer and Phoebe Stabler's
sister; Charles Noke, Art Director of Doulton's; and Alfred and
Louise Powell, who worked both independently and with Wedgwood's. The model for the Design and Industries Association was
the Deutscher Werkbund, founded in Germany in 1907. By 1915
the Werkbund was an extremely influential body and in Britain,
despite the war, a group of English artists and craftsmen persuaded
the Board of Trade to allow an exhibition of German design in the
Goldsmiths' Hall in London. The D.I.A. was founded two months
later and one of its first publications was devoted to extolling its
German model. Basing their views on the German, the D.I.A.
Council and members quickly established a philosophy. Their
basic principle was that 'The first necessity of sound design is

fitness for use', and the slogan 'Fitness for use' or 'Fitness for purpose' became the Association's battle-cry.[5]

The British Institute of Industrial Art was the government-backed counterpart organization. It was set up in 1919 with a Treasury grant, but after the 1921 slump was left to become self-supporting. Its aims were much the same as those of the D.I.A., with the added bonus of an established connection with the Victoria and Albert Museum, where the Institute's own collection of industrial design was housed.

Although neither organization was as influential as the Werkbund, membership nevertheless meant that the Stablers brought with them contacts with some of the most important and useful men of their time.

John Adams studied at Hanley School of Art. He left school at the age of thirteen, joined the design studio of a tile-producing firm and studied at the local art school in evening classes, as did so many of the Poole employees twenty years later. In his early twenties he joined the decoration studio of Bernard Moore, which specialized in *flambé* and lustre painting. In 1908 he won one of the ten National Scholarships to study at the Royal College of Art and so came to London. Hanley at this time had no facilities for firing pottery, and the glazed faience and other pieces with which students hoped to win awards, were sent for firing to Woolliscroft's tile works or Wardle's factory at Shelton. This type of sculptural work was the strongest subject at Hanley. According to John Adams it was the source of many National Competition awards. The tradition was inherited from the style of teaching established under the influence of continental sculptors such as Carrier-Belleuse and Hughues Protat, both of whom worked for Minton's around 1850.[6]

Working and studying in London was an enriching experience for John Adams:

To live with a friend in two rooms in Chelsea or Fulham 'doing for yourselves', with the river trying hard to look like a Whistler Nocturne; to go to a primitive moving-picture house to see for the first time 'a funny little devil called Charlie Chaplin'; to watch from the gallery of Covent Garden (one shilling) the incomparable Russian dancers Nijinski and Kharsavina with the decor of Bakst's *L'ápres-midi d'un Faune*:[7] to sit among the enormous red-coated guardsmen in the Chelsea Palace listening to that great little artist, Albert Chevalier, singing about his 'Old Dutch',

Dish, painted in purple, pinks and greens, an adaptation by
Truda Carter of the Grape pattern by Erna Manners. 1921–4.
Victoria & Albert Museum.

and they with a tear in the eye, ready to start a rough-house if anyone
was so indiscreet as to notice it; to drift home across the quiet well-bred
squares of South Kensington; all that was an essential part of a young
artist's experience which not even Stoke nor the Royal College, valuable
as they were, could excel.[8]

Opportunities for work and study also opened out. In 1912
Adams, with three other Potteries students at the Royal College,
Fred S. Harrop, Arthur Scott and Reginald R. Tomlinson, spent
two months working on the decorations for the Palace of Peace at
The Hague, designing wall tiling, stained glass, embroidered hangings and figures. Adams and another student were responsible for
the gilded reliefs covering the vaulting over the main entrance.
Like every other student in London, John Adams also took advantage of the close proximity of the Victoria and Albert Museum's
collections. As he himself commented:

View of a display, probably at the Gieves Gallery, *c.* 1923, showing: Blue Stripe
ware; left: an ovoid vase probably with a Chinese Blue or similar glaze; back left:
the Spotted Deer design by Truda Carter on a dish; back right: a modelled plaque
by Harold Stabler, one of a series based on seasonal flowers; two figures by
Phoebe Stabler, below, the 'Buster Boy' and above, the 'Piping Boy'. *Poole Pottery Ltd.*

Child's plate, designed by Dora Batty, painted in purples, black, blue and yellow
by Ruth Pavely. This design was also used on tiles in the Nursery Toys series.
c. 1922. *Private collection.*

View of an exhibition held at Regent House in 1921, showing a dish by Truda
Carter, Blue Stripe ware and Truda Carter's floral designs. *Poole Pottery Ltd.*

The Museum has always played an important part in the designer's training. There he can find examples of almost every known ceramic decorative process done by master hands. The young potter can match himself against those old masters and find books and priceless historic manuscripts in the Museum Library that give details of various techniques. Bernard Rackham was the Keeper of Ceramics when I studied in the Museum Galleries, and I have grateful memories of his unfailing courtesy in taking a specimen out of the glass case to examine its material, or to discuss the qualities of workmanship and, for want of a better word, its surface 'texture'.[9]

This last comment is particularly interesting in the light of contact between the two men in later years, when John Adams was involved in arranging for the exhibition of pottery at the Museum.

After he had completed the three-year course, Adams remained at the Royal College, on the staff, and during this time he met and married Gertrude (Truda) Sharp, a fellow ARCA. In 1914 they moved to South Africa where he took up the position of Head of the School of Art at the Durban Technical College. He and Truda established the pottery section at the College but, in spite of this and other contributions to the system, when the Adamses came to England on a holiday in about 1920 or 1921 they were disillusioned with art education in South Africa and consequently ripe for Harold Stabler to persuade them to join the Poole venture.

In addition to Stabler and the Adamses' arrival in 1921, Benjamin Evelyn Elford, the company secretary, was appointed to the Board in 1917 and Cyril joined in 1919 on his return from the war. Elford had been with the firm from 1898 at least.[10] He became managing director and chairman (a post which always combined the two titles) and on Charles' retirement in 1928 he took on the major administrative role. For two decades he played an important part on the managerial side of the business during its formative period and the years of establishment. He retired in 1947.

In the first years of the new company fresh staff were appointed. When Margaret Holder joined in November 1921 she became the fourth paintress. The others were Anne Hatchard, who had been with Carter's since 1918; Sissy Collet, who had been working with James Radley Young for nine years (she left in 1922), had designed some early sprig patterns and had trained Anne Hatchard; and a Miss Kendall. Early in 1922 other paintresses were taken on including Ruth Pavely, who began work in February 1922.[11] By

Dish, painted colours, designed by Truda Carter and illustrated in the *Design & Industries Association Yearbook, 1922. Private collection.*

1924 there were ten paintresses.[12] Most of these educated and artistic girls were selected by John Adams. Margaret Holder, for instance, studied at Bournemouth Art School where her work for the Sketch Club was singled out by John Adams. She trained in lithography and illustration and when she was taken on by the Pottery she specialized in lettering. Ruth Pavely who, like Margaret Holder before her, became head of the painting department, had been intended by her parents to become a violin teacher. She opposed this plan and so her father, who knew Cyril Carter, arranged for her introduction to the Pottery and the two were taken around the works. Her description of conditions at that time are graphic. It was dark and dirty, there was no proper plumbing

Vase, pattern designed by Truda Carter and painted in greens, purples and yellow by Anne Hatchard. Lettering painted by Margaret Holder. The Bourne Revellers were a concert party which included Anne Hatchard as contralto (the party members' names are on the base). Captain Norton was a local merchant. 1924.
Victoria & Albert Museum.

and you found your coat in the cloakroom by touch.[13] By this time installed at a desk in his father's office, Cyril instigated several improvements in staff accommodation, including better lavatories to replace the one two-seater unit which had previously served the whole East Quay factory.[14]

Almost immediately, with the setting up of C.S.A. and the influx of new staff, the Pottery began to produce new and different wares. Truda Adams made the first impression on the Pottery's output with the introduction of a range of floral patterns. Building on the basic style of painted sprigs and floral sprays begun by J.R.Y., she developed a range of freshly and brightly coloured over-all decoration within a rich and yet carefully controlled palette. These

designs were adapted to fit the different shapes by the senior
paintresses, such as Margaret Holder, subject to Truda's approval;
the junior staff then prepared paper pounces. Paintresses were on
piecework and paid 1s. for a dozen sprigs or bands painted; vertical
stripes which were difficult were 2s. a dozen.[15] The clay body of
the pots at this time varied between the grey-buff previously used,
a red earthenware and also occasionally a grey-brown or brown
body fired almost to a stoneware temperature. Whatever the basic
body colour all the wares were covered with a slip. This, in the
earliest days, was a thick grey-white but was quickly improved to
a warmer, clearer creamy-white.

While Truda was the resident designer and provided the vast
majority of these patterns, visiting artists also contributed. Since
John Adams and particularly Harold Stabler had lively contacts
with the design world and the Royal College, it was to be expected
that students or friends of the two men should frequently provide
patterns for the paintresses. Many of these people may have visited
Poole for a brief weekend in 1921 or 1922, sketched a few ideas
and never returned. The sketches were absorbed into the Poole
range, adapted and altered until they became part of the house
style, and the tenuous link with the original author was lost completely. It is difficult to identify many of these visiting friends, and
impossible to guess at the people who never came to Poole at all
but simply met Stabler or Adams in London over dinner and
dashed off an idea or two. Stabler was probably chiefly responsible
for this lively and valuable injection of contemporary ideas, since
it was he who brought in several students directly from the Royal
College. Erna Manners was one such RCA student who worked for
a short time at the Pottery and designed the 'Grape' and 'Fuchsia'
patterns.[16] Among others were Irene Fawkes and Olive Bourne.
Irene Fawkes also designed a catalogue cover about 1930, and
Olive Bourne specialized during the 1930s in pottery designs based
on female figures and heads in stylized classical style. In addition,
undoubtedly, John Adams revived many friendships on his return
to England with people only too keen to try their hand at pottery
decoration or a little modelling. Cyril, an outgoing and sociable
man by nature with cosmopolitan views developed by his experi-
ences during the war in India and in Egypt, was, like Stabler, in
contact with most of the design associations. He too was partly
responsible for the stream of visitors to the works. Even the pain-

tresses stepped outside their role as decorators and were allowed not only to interpret established patterns but also to offer original designs for Truda's approval. Since many of them were trained artists in their own right this was only natural.

Amid this sudden burst of creative production generated in the decorating shop, the unglazed ware begun by J.R.Y. was also continued. On a closer, buff-coloured, high-fired body the painting became smoother and smarter. The range of shapes increased considerably to include footed tazzas, mugs, covered bowls and jars, and in the quality and fineness of production they reflect the growing expertise of the Pottery's throwers. Lily Gilham, trained as she had been under J.R.Y. to make varied and individual wares, never adapted to the necessarily standard and uniform requirements of a pottery intent on mass production of high artistic quality while achieving commercial success. However, her younger sister Gertrude (Gertie) was much more adaptable and became C.S.A.'s chief thrower. She taught the skill at the local art school and in later years occupied a star position on the route taken by visitors through the works.

Photographic records of shapes were kept in 1921. Dorothea

Fruit dish, painted in blue, yellow, greens and purples with a pattern designed by Truda Carter. 1921–5. *Private collection.*

Two-handled vase, painted in blues, purples, yellow and green, Flying Bird
pattern, designed by Truda Carter. 1921–5. *Victoria & Albert Museum.*

Salamon, who was on C.S.A.'s staff and whose sister Lola married
Roger Carter's twin brother Harry, took the photographs. However, the difficulties of indicating precise measurements and the
thrower's need for a clearer outline led them to adopt the system
of profile and section drawings used by other potteries. This work
was given to Margaret Holder, who allotted a number to the
design, took the measurements and made a drawing in the Shapes
Book. A second drawing on stout card (afterwards varnished) was
made for the throwing shops. John Adams approved the drawing
before she inked them in.[17]

John Adams' particular contribution, also begun in these early
years, was in the field of glaze experiment. Adams was what has
been described by several of his colleagues as an 'art school',
intuitive potter. He had many years' experience in and around the

pottery industry, particularly on the decorating side. However, in 1921 he began to experiment, with the aid of the Poole technicians, in glaze techniques and effects. With the occasional contribution from Harold Stabler he began designing new shapes for vases, jars and covered bowls, with a range of semi-matt to glossy glazes in blues, browns and black, brilliant orange and white.

Many of these glazes were directly based on developments made by individual studio potters using wood ash and other natural ingredients – Ernest Legg has mentioned rhododendron wood ash for instance.[18] Other glazes imitated these effects. In contrast, those purely chemical or metal-based glazes included not only the brilliant uranium-based orange, which every pottery intent on sales and a progressive reputation was obliged to produce from the mid-1920s, but also a group of dazzling Chinese and Persian Blues, the latter with a crackled appearance controlled in the firing. These glazes demanded the development of a stoneware body and in time a very fine dense material of the highest quality was made.

In effect Adams had produced a range which filled the slot previously occupied by Owen Carter's lustre glazes; a range of 'art' pots designed to attract the more knowledgeable and artistic customer. When the lustres were discontinued as too *Art Nouveau* and dated, the Chinese Blues, Tangerines and Mirror Blacks became the modern equivalent. Many of these pieces and the larger painted wares were sold with a black wood stand, carved in the Chinese manner.[19] Chinese Blue, slipware and plain brown-glazed pieces were shown at the British Institute of Industrial Art exhibition held at the Whitworth Institute Art Galleries in Manchester in 1924.[20]

The sales outlet through Liberty's, established before the war by Carter & Co., stood C.S.A. in good stead during the 1920s, despite the continuing anonymity upon which the retailers insisted. Further contacts were made, most importantly with Heal's, the arbiters of discriminating and forward-looking ideas in design. In 1921, the first year of their production, C.S.A. showed their wares at the British Industries Fair at Olympia. The stand was designed by Heal's and was packed with pots, including a number of large covered jars decorated with the new Blue Stripe patterns. Phoebe Stabler's figure of 'The Piping Boy', and the roundel 'The Piping, or Dancing, Faun' were also shown. The following year they again exhibited the same figures plus several new ones, at the first exhi-

Bowl, decorated with combed slip trailing possibly by Jim Soper, probably designed by John Adams. 1922–3. *Victoria & Albert Museum.*

bition held at the Victoria and Albert Museum by the British Institute of Industrial Art. The enlarged range included 'The Picardy Peasant', 'The Flower Girl' and 'The Little Shepherd', with two others simply recorded as 'Girl' and 'Boy'.[21] Unfortunately there are no illustrations to help with identification of these figures, whose individual titles vary slightly with each exhibition and which, in any case, are so confusingly similar. 'The Flower Girl' in another exhibition could become 'The Lavender Woman', while 'The Little Shepherd' could become the 'Piping Boy'.

The British Industries Fair was held every February and C.S.A. exhibited there regularly. In 1923, with the Tileworks, they contributed to the Architectural Pottery, Art Pottery, Earthenware, Fancies, Teapots and Jugs, and Tiles sections, also advertising in the catalogue 'exceptional pieces for collectors'.[22]

In addition C.S.A. held annual exhibitions at the Gieves Gallery in London each September. The stands were arranged in elaborate 'still life' settings and photographs of them were used as frontispieces for the catalogues which the Pottery issued from 1921. One

Vase, painted in greens, yellow, blue, purples and black with a pattern designed by Truda Carter. 1925–30. *Victoria & Albert Museum.*

exception was an early booklet entitled *Pottery Making at Poole*, in which a simple account of the history and manufacturing process, probably written by Cyril Carter, was illustrated with charming and witty vignettes by Edward Bawden. At the time Bawden was still a student at the Royal College and like so many others was persuaded by Harold Stabler to contribute towards the Poole venture, in his case in the form of these illustrations and also with some designs for the Tileworks. In keeping with their retail outlets through the more progressive and prestigious London stores, C.S.A. also had their catalogues and brochures printed at the Curwen Press. Again Cyril Carter and Harold Stabler were probably jointly responsible for this choice of one of the most enlightened printers of the day.

Cyril, in company with the Pottery's new partners, was very much involved in the design and art world; he followed developments in the pottery industry and was closely aware of discussions and trends. In October 1921 he joined a debate in the *Pottery Gazette and Glass Trade Review*. The debate was opened with an address given by Gordon Forsyth at the quarterly meeting of the National Pottery Council at the North Staffordshire Hotel in Stoke-on-Trent. Forsyth, that great figure in twentieth-century ceramic decoration and philosophy, claimed that:

It was only by art that the pottery industry would gain fresh ground and find new fields to conquer. The application of sound artistic ideals had a direct and immediate effect upon the industry, and what one desired to see was honest English art allied to English pottery: something in the nature of a co-operative effort to abolish artistic affectation. . . . The artist or designer . . . should have imagination, a thorough knowledge of processes and methods of pottery decoration (which naturally includes a thorough knowledge of historical styles) and last, but not least, a real veneration for his craft.[23]

The debate continued in the *Gazette* for the next two months, inspiring letters from a representative of Camberwell School of Art and Crafts in September and Cyril Carter in October. Cyril took the opportunity to attack what, obviously, was a particular irritant to him – the prefix 'art' which for decades had been applied to every conceivable object from decorative ceramic wares to household ironmongery.

Sirs, – The great pottery industry of this country seems to be taking itself very seriously just at present. Having taken unto itself an Art Director, he appears to be getting to work with great vigour. 'Only by Art', Mr. Forsyth tells the potters, 'will the industry gain fresh ground and find new fields to conquer'. He tells them, too, that what we want is something in the nature of a co-operative effort for the abolition of artistic affectation, but says that it is quite impossible to lay down any hard and fast rule for Art. Now, to an ignorant tile-maker who is not supposed to be concerned with art to the same extent as the 'real' potter, all this is rather bewildering. For although at the back of my mind I have a feeling that somewhere in the country there is an 'Art Tile Works', Art would appear to be no new thing to the general potter. Looking through the advertisement pages of the trade papers one is led to believe that the pottery industry is glutted with Art. Half the potters in the country seem to make 'Art' pottery, and some go one better and make 'Fine Art' pottery.

Perhaps that is the trouble, that there is too much Art – always with the large A – and too little honesty of purpose. We tile-makers are not guiltless in this matter, as we have certain colours which we call 'Art' colours and which are consequently more expensive. If Mr. Forsyth can induce us to think a little less about Art as a name and a little more about making honest pottery, fitted in every way to the purpose for which it is made, one cannot help feeling we shall be moving in the right direction. 'Art' and 'Artists' are dangerous words to play with. The sanitary ware maker who turns out a really well made porcelain bath doesn't call it an 'Art Bath', but there is probably more art in its composition than in all the pottery cats with long necks and the clock sets and other 'shooting gallery' stuff that Staffordshire devotes its great mind to turning out.

Mr. Forsyth's vision of the really capable designer gulching out enough designs (!) in three months to keep the potter going for a year reminds one of Shelley's skylark, for one sees him ('blithe spirit' that he will be with three months work a year to look forward to), one sees him, as he

'From 'Stoke', or near it,
Poureth his full heart
In profuse strains
of unpremeditated art.'

In the meantime, if Mr. Forsyth cannot lay down any hard-and-fast rule for Art, perhaps he might be able to give us a ruling about 'Art Pottery',

Yours, etc.,   Poole Pottery, Poole, Dorset
Cyril Carter   Sept. 5 1921[24]

   This letter gives a great deal of insight into Cyril Carter's think-
ing at this time and also accurately reflects the Poole philosophy.
There has always been a certain sensitivity on the part of the Poole
potters towards the Staffordshire potteries. Directly in competition,
particularly on the tile-making side, Poole and Hamworthy found
the pride which the Stoke-on-Trent potters had for their past,
insular and difficult to accept when imported south. Skilled people
had come to Dorset from Stoke and many had settled and contributed to the growth of the two potteries, John Adams being a prime
example. But this was not always the case and a little of the
resultant defensiveness appears in Cyril's letter. Apart from this
particular idiosyncrasy, however, the main opinion expressed is
based soundly on those D.I.A. principles formed in 1915.

   Cyril was a member of the D.I.A. and had by 1921 fully
absorbed the Association's tenets. C.S.A. production was made
under this philosophy and aimed at D.I.A.-minded customers. The
Pottery's aims were set out in one of their earliest catalogues,
published in about 1922, the introduction written by the journalist
and D.I.A. member Joseph Thorp.

Every trace of the affectation of 'peasant art' (a danger incident to the
handcraft potter) that may have crept in is rigorously eliminated. Pots
already made have been passed in review, and some (I rejoice to record)
have been ruthlessly smashed as not coming up to the potters' exacting
standard of practical serviceability: in particular, some that were graceful
enough in appearance, but so narrowly based as to be in danger of being
overset by a careless touch, or, when filled with flowers, by a gusty
draught. This seems to me not only good art, but good, enlightened
business.

   The new direction is carrying on and developing the making of domestic ware. And here C.S.A. – and it is a good instance of the sanity of
their outlook – feel that it is not only legitimate but necessary to depart
from the ideal of hand-throwing. Qualities of 'freedom of drawing' which
are the beauty of a pot or bowl are an affectation in a teacup. One simply
does not want to drink tea out of an 'art pot'. It is done, I know, but not
by 'the best people'! The intimate things of the table should, so C.S.A.
feel, be as *neatly* made and smoothly finished as possible, and when the
machine 'jolly' will achieve this the jolly will be used.

   Beauty of shape, interest of texture and glazing, will not be sacrificed;
while the decoration will be honest brush-work – not transfers which give
such a relatively melancholy and stereotyped effect. I have in a previous
notice of these Poole products pointed out that the public has been eager

Vase, glazed inside, with decoration in browns, probably adapted by Truda Carter from designs by James Radley Young and painted by Ruth Pavely. *c.* 1930. *Victoria & Albert Museum.*

to buy where the 'buyers' of the retail shops and stores have (often at first reluctantly) been prevailed upon to give people a chance to see this beautiful ware.[25]

Both this catalogue and the next were well illustrated with black-and-white and coloured photographs and included detailed price lists. In 1923 Thorp summed up the progress made in the first year and a half.

It has been a year of consolidation, of constant experiment and research, of substantial technical progress, and, I am happy to say in view of

certain prophecies I had hazarded, a year of great encouragement from
the business point of view.

These potters have been frequently assured by candid friends that there
is only a very limited public for such wares. Their own belief, and mine
– I will admit it sometimes looked a little against the weight of evidence
– was that there was quite a sufficient, and what was more important, a
steadily growing public which wanted lovely things, not in the collector's
spirit of acquisitiveness and artificial scarcity value, but for use in daily
life, things to the making of which had gone intelligence, appreciation of
purpose, honest respect for material, rigid eschewing of any 'arty' affectation, and real feeling for and desire to create, however humbly, real
beauty.

Well, the verdict of the croakers, 'Very charming and creditable to
you, but impracticable from a business point of view,' has gone by the
board. These lovely pots actually sell – they really do – out of ordinary
shops to ordinary people in ordinary houses.[26]

These introductions give an interesting idea of one member's
interpretation of the D.I.A. principles. Thorp's version was almost
romantic and certainly not entirely an accurate representation. In
D.I.A. terms it was not possible to make a pot that looked good
or graceful if it was unbalanced or unsteady. The two attributes
would have been indivisible in D.I.A. eyes. Undoubtedly the
C.S.A. management saw themselves in a similar light – a curious
combination of high, even romantic ideas, combined with an
undeniable amount of shrewd business sense – more than Thorp
realized – as demonstrated in Cyril's letter to the *Pottery Gazette
and Glass Trade Review*. Despite Thorp's claim about ordinary shops
and ordinary customers, Poole's most important buyers away from
the local area, were Liberty's, Heal's and other fairly exclusive
stores in London and elsewhere, and these were their proudest
advertisement. In the 1923 catalogue, Phoebe Stabler's figures sold
from 12s. 6d. for 'The Bath Towel' through £2 10s. for a single
'Picardy Peasant' to £6 6s. for 'The Bull'. Large 'pots' of around
10 or 11 in. in height sold for two or three guineas depending on
the amount of painted decoration. General domestic ware, most of
it with painted decoration, was priced at 9d. for an eggcup to 15s.
6d. for an eight-piece morning tea set, simply decorated with single
flowers springing from circular bands of colours. Pieces covered
with the Chinese Blue or other glaze effects compared favourably
in price with the painted wares. A Chinese Blue 'floating bowl',
$10\frac{3}{8}$ in. in diameter, was priced at 15s., while a similar shape,

Two kitchen storage jars, the lettering cut through blue slip to the white body beneath by Margaret Holder. *c. 1927. Victoria & Albert Museum.*

13½ in. in diameter, but with painted decoration, cost £1 5s. They may have sold; but it was not until the 1930s that they really sold in quantity, and throughout the 1920s and 1930s they were supported by the far more successful Tileworks.

In 1925 C.S.A. were represented by a large selection of wares at the International Exhibition of Modern Decorative and Industrial Art in Paris. This included various previously exhibited figures by the Stablers and some newly modelled pieces such as the 'Fighting Cock', 'The Harpy Eagle' (shown in the Garden Statuary Section) and 'large blue pots', probably also garden wares. Groups of vases, pots and jars were also shown. In addition to the Stabler statuary normally sold through the C.S.A. catalogues, the Tileworks also contributed Della Robbia ware.[27] The works were awarded a *Diplôme d'Honneur* and a gold medal, and the art and technical side were also awarded a *Diplôme d'Honneur* and gold, silver and bronze medals. This achievement was used as advertising material in the form of a printed handout probably designed by Dora Batty, another of Harold Stabler's Royal College of Art contacts and a

Bowl, Plane ware, in white, designed by John Adams, the handles glazed with
Sapphire or Powder Blue. *c.* 1935. *Victoria & Albert Museum.*

student-contemporary of Edward Bawden. She made designs for
both the Pottery and the Tileworks, specializing in nursery scenes
based on children's rhymes. Nursery tableware was produced in
quantity with a choice of names lettered around the edge.

These awards in Paris were a major success for a pottery in the
comparatively early stages of its development; they set a seal of
approval on the aspirations of the company. During the next few
years the technical and artistic achievements of the mid-decade
were crystallized into a more positive and individual pottery line,
increasingly successful in design and production. In 1927 they
contributed to the 'very satisfactory'[28] British section of the International Exhibition of Industrial Art at Leipzig. This was organ-
ized by the Design and Industries Association and C.S.A. showed
Harold and Phoebe Stabler faience – a galleon and the 'Piping
Faun' roundel – with some of the large decorated vases, which had
been described as representing 'one of the firm's strongholds'.[29]
Their stand, flanked with textiles by the notable designers Marion
Dorn, Phyllis Barron and Dorothy Larcher, showed the production
of a decade at the highest point of achievement.

5
1930-1939

Carter, Stabler & Adams: tableware, standardization and exhibitions

BY the end of the 1920s and in the early 1930s, like every other pottery, C.S.A. had been influenced by the stylistic trends emanating from the French contribution to the 1925 Exhibition. Scathingly referred to as Jazz Modern by the purists of the time, and now known by the more modern term Art Deco, the C.S.A. version began with angular, geometric patterns in the continental or French style on their own previously established shapes. Thus they made a good, serviceable, traditional jug shape and decorated it with a lively, modernistic pattern. The painted patterns in this style were generally distinguished from the more garish attempts of other contemporary potteries by their restrained colouring; undoubtedly Truda had a very accurate and discerning eye for colour combinations. John Adams too was affected by the French influence and he began designing new shapes to take the range of coloured glazes he had developed. Harold Stabler also contributed fresh ideas in the form of angular, faceted vases relieved with decorative beading, which were first put into production as early as 1925 or 1926. Another range, introduced in about 1930, was known as Plane Ware and consisted mainly, if not entirely, of vases. These were plainly glazed and decorated with applied flange-type wings, or handles, set asymmetrically. By this time wares which were part of a named range were generally printed with that name, in addition to the printed pattern or glaze code, the impressed pottery backstamp, the incised shape number and, where applicable, the paintress's insignia. Curiously the two areas of modernistic design provided by Truda Carter and John Adams never really coincided, and the more jazzy, painted patterns were not applied to the equivalent in shape design, which instead was reserved for glaze decoration.

Around 1930 Carter & Co.'s red clay pits began to run out and a white body was introduced into the Pottery. For a few years C.S.A. tried to disguise this fact, presumably concerned at the effect the different colour might have on the appearance of their wares and possibly also on the buying public. Whatever the reason, they covered the basic white body with a red slip and then overlaid that with the white slip which they had always used over the original red body. The difference this procedure made to the outward decorated surface is an unreliable guide to dating, owing to

Jug, decoration designed by Truda Carter, painted in sepia, grey, blue and black by Ruth Pavely. 1932–5. *Private collection.*

the density and variable colour of the white slip. However, it is quite obvious from the underside of the ware because any turned foot rim, incised or impressed mark is cut through the two slip layers to the white body. Nevertheless there are examples even from the 1950s which have a pink stain added to the slip or glaze inside some jars and pots, a remaining vestige of this practice.

The number of glazes was extended in 1932 to include the Picotee range of sprayed colours applied in rings around the body of the ware and named after a type of carnation. As with any new technique, the initial conception was that of John Adams, whose passion for gardening is reflected in the choice of name, and the development was carried out by the relevant technician. In this

Plate, decoration painted in black, yellow, blue and pink, designed by Olive Bourne. 1930–35. *Poole Pottery Ltd. Photograph: Victoria & Albert Museum.*

case Leslie Elsden, head of the spraying shop, carried through the necessary experiments and perfected the final technique. Spraying was used extensively not only for Picotee ware but also for a range of table and decorative pieces known as Everest ware. This was introduced by 1933, and the raised, stepped bands, which were the distinguishing feature, were additionally decorated with sprayed coloured glazes. Ornaments and figures were also spray-glazed.

In about 1935 the Sylvan glaze range was introduced; this described a group of mottled colours with the code numbers M7, M22, M24, M36, M38, M70 and M72. The colours range from a mixture of black and orange, through orange and yellow, yellow and green to yellow and blue. They were applied to existing decorative shapes – vases, plant pots, posy rings, candlesticks, ashtrays, inkstands and so on – and were an alternative to the existing pastel and other plain shades. A leaflet was issued to advertise their introduction.

INDIVIDUAL CHARACTER and liveliness of form are only present when the pot is handmade. These pieces of SYLVAN WARE are made entirely by hand at the Old Pottery on the QUAY at Poole in DORSET. They are amongst the extremely few wares now-a-days which are genuinely hand-thrown without the use of moulds or profiles. The shapes are varied, and their range is constantly being added to. They are covered with semi-matt glazes of exquisite quality, and there is a wide choice of colour. Besides the broken effects they are produced in plain MAGNOLIA WHITE, APPLE GREEN, PASTEL PINK, PASTEL BLUE, & PASTEL GREY. The outline sketches opposite show only a small proportion of the designs available.[1]

A few experimental pieces also survive from this period. For instance, the Pottery owns in its collection the figure of a fish which is covered with a clear, crackled, semi-matt glaze, slightly tinged with green and blue. This, with the Persian Blue mentioned earlier, represents work done on glaze firing techniques which apparently never became a significant part of production at the Pottery, although crackled glazes were certainly produced in some quantity at the Tileworks.

Pursuing the Design and Industries Association image and in comparison with the more jazzy patterned ware (itself distinct from the traditional floral designs), C.S.A. also produced a range of discreetly white- and cream-glazed decorative items. These vases, bowls and dishes were intended to appeal to the design-conscious

Vase, moulded, gadrooned shape, designed by Owen Carter. Dated 1904. *Poole Pottery Ltd.*

Vase, moulded, panelled shape, designed by Owen Carter. Dated 1905. *Poole Pottery Ltd.*

Dish, possibly painted by Ja[...]
Radley Young, the rim deco[...]
apparently influenced by the[...]
of Vanessa Bell. It has been
suggested that the view is of[...]
Castle. *c.* 1914–20. *Poole Pott[...]*

'The Bull', designed by Har[...]
and Phoebe Stabler, made a[...]
sold by Carter, Stabler & A[...]
Ltd throughout the 1920s ar[...]
early 1930s. 1914. *Victoria &*
Museum.

Vase, designed by Truda C[...]
and painted by Ruth Pavely
c. 1926. *Private collection.*

Jar and cover, with Chinese Blue glaze, designed by John Adams. c. 1925–30. *Poole Pottery Ltd.*

Vase, with speckled stoneware glaze, designed by John Adams and fired by Ernest Legg. c. 1935. *Private collection.*

otee ware, designed by John Adams and spray
ed probably by Leslie Elsden. *c.* 1932. *Private*
ction.

e, probably designed by Truda Carter. *c.* 1930.
e Pottery Ltd.

ıp of tiles, Waterbirds, designed by Harold Stabler. *c.* 1921–5. *Victoria & Albert Museum.*

ıp of tiles. Left: Seagull, possibly designed by Irene Fawkes; centre: Caller Herrin', designed by Dora M.
y; right: Fishing Smacks, designed by Minnie McLeish. 1921–5. *Victoria & Albert Museum.*

Durban War Memorial, designed by
. G. Pilkington and modelled by
ıld Stabler. 1925. *Pilkington Tiles Ltd.*

Dish, designed by Robert Jefferson. 1965. *Private collection.*

Carter, Stabler & Adams Ltd postcard showing Ruth Pavely decorating a vase. *c.* 1936. *Leslie Elsden.*

connoisseur whose taste leaned more towards what was known as the International Modern movement, that is the north European, German or Scandinavian style, directly opposed to the Jazz Modern trends. This area of custom was typified by Heal's, in whose illustrated catalogues C.S.A. production figured largely. Heal's catered for the basically Arts and Crafts-minded client with a modern bent, and in their room setting of simple yet stylish oak furniture they featured Poole faience – Phoebe and Harold Stabler figures and galleons – on the one hand, and on the other the new range of cool, muted wares entitled Magnolia and Polar White. As with all design aspects of Poole production, outside artists frequently contributed and in this case the range was added to by Harry Trethowan, the chief pottery buyer for Heal's, in what was obviously a mutually satisfactory arrangement. Another Heal's connection of significance was that with the architect Sir Edward Maufe, who designed Cyril Carter's house, 'Yaffle Hill', completed in 1932. Lady Maufe was on the board of Heal's directors.

In 1936 a large private commission for a dinner service was received from a Mr and Mrs Watkinson of South Africa. Possibly there was an old connection from the Adamses' time in Durban, although by this date Truda and John Adams were divorced (she had married Cyril Carter in about 1931). The commission was for

THE LATEST DEVELOPMENT OF

POOLE POTTERY
THE NEW
"PICOTEE WARE"
MADE IN
MANY SHAPES
AND
COLOURINGS
BY

CARTER, STABLER AND ADAMS LTD.
POTTERS, POOLE, DORSET.

Advertisement for Carter, Stabler & Adams Ltd Picotee ware, from the *Pottery Gazette & Glass Trade Review Diary, 1933.*

a design by Truda of a simple, individual flower in buffs, browns and greys, the rims edged with a single grey line. It was not the first time the Pottery had manufactured dinner ware, but for this special individual order they had no means of producing the required flatware. A unique set was too expensive in time and equipment and so they purchased the blanks from Pountney of Bristol.[2] The decoration was painted by Ruth Pavely.

Previous to this commission they had made a certain amount of domestic tableware sets, most notably the coffee and tea sets designed by Harold Stabler and used in the Pottery visitors' tea-rooms. These rooms were opened in 1933 and were designed by the architect Howard Robertson. Not only visitors were catered for; the tea-rooms functioned as an unofficial club where Cyril, Harold Stabler and John Adams met and discussed the current Pottery affairs. The tea-rooms were presided over by Maggie Purdie, a cousin of Truda's, who was famed for her shortcake.[3] The tea and coffee sets, in a style derived from Stabler's silver work, were known as Studland and were spray-glazed in Apple Green, and also blue, either Powder Blue or Sapphire Blue.[4] The Studland ware enjoyed a certain exclusive success; it was shown in various prestigious exhibitions and illustrated in the more important trade journals, as was the Picotee tableware also designed in the same year. However, following the Watkinson commission John Adams turned his mind to the necessity of introducing a competitive standard ware. He designed the Pottery's first major breakthrough in the domestic line, the Streamline shape, which was first made with a variation of the Watkinson pattern. Not only was this the first commercial success but it was also their most successful tableware and was continued after the war with various small adaptations. The introduction of this new shape coincided with the development by Ernest Baggaley of the two colour combination glazes with a Vellum semi-matt finish. Baggaley was brought in from Stoke-on-Trent by John Adams at the beginning of 1936. He had trained at Stoke Technical College and, in his own words, his appointment at Poole was to counter-balance a situation in which C.S.A.'s artistic ability had outrun their technical ability. He threw the first Streamline shapes but his particular achievement was the standardizing of bodies and glazes, and these combination glazes were a first development. The introductory pair of colours were Sepia and Mushroom and the range was quickly expanded to

Vase, Everest ware, in white, black and muted buff shades, designed by John Adams. *c.* 1935. *Victoria & Albert Museum.*

include Seagull (a mottled grey), Peach, Ice Green and Lime, in various combinations. After the Second World War this style of paired colours was given the range name of Twintone.[5]

After the standard tableware had been introduced and established as part of the Poole range, the decorative wares were not only continued but also developed. In about 1931 a series of plates was started, each decorated with painted views of accurately detailed sailing ships. A local portrait artist, Arthur Bradbury, who was interested in boats, brought in some drawings of ships to John Adams. Bradbury had trained at the St John's Wood Art School in London and then at the Royal Academy.[6] The drawings he offered were accepted, to be set in the centre of large dishes whose rims and lettering would be painted by Margaret Holder.[7] The centres of these special plates were done by the more senior paintresses who included Margaret Holder herself and Ruth Pavely. This series showing boats of local and historical interest achieved lasting popularity and is still produced today, with some variations. Probably all the ships were either built at Poole or used the harbour regularly. The range is listed in a handwritten note in

Vase, designed by John Adams, with black handles, the body covered with mottled semi-matt black, blue and green glazes. *c.* 1935. *Victoria & Albert Museum.*

the Pottery records as the '*James* 1386, *Harry Paye*, late 14th century, *Primrose*, 1588, *Sea Adventure*, 1694, HM Sloop, *Viper*, 1746 (built at Poole), *Poole Whaler*, 1783, *General Wolfe*, 1797 (Newfoundland trader), *Igeia*, yacht, built at Poole, 1871, Poole Trawler *Polly*, built at Poole, 1906.' The *Waterwitch*, a barquentine on which Bradbury sailed as a merchant seaman, was a favourite subject which he also depicted in watercolours. A few years later, in 1936, another set of plates decorated with Poole harbour subjects was produced experimentally. These were probably designed by Leslie Ward, head of Bournemouth Art School. His designs were sent into the Pottery and were given by John Adams to Margaret Holder to convert into something closer to the recognizable Poole style. However, they were never developed to Adams' satisfaction and only one set was made. Of this set one plate is known, in the Pottery's own collection, and shows a view of Poole quay with sailing boats, painted in blue and edged around the rim in yellow.[8]

Phoebe Stabler's figures appear to have been dropped, gradually, in the early thirties and others took their place. John Adams made some designs partly of purely ornamental pieces and partly of useful items, such as candlesticks which incorporated a strong decorative element. The basic design for these in particular used a favourite decorative feature, a grape-laden vine, very Jazz Modern in style. This was first produced around 1930, still close enough to the Paris International Exhibition of 1925 to show the French influence. Several variations on the initial theme were made ranging from single to three-branch candlesticks, sold individually or in pairs. This vine motif was also adapted for use as decorative handles on vases and a supporting pedestal to love-birds or doves. As with the candlesticks, the dove group was made either as a free-standing ornament or, with some adaptations, for use as a book-end. Once the first motif was established, it was adapted, altered and re-thought for different uses and combinations. While John Adams made the initial design, the subsequent developments and modelling were done by Harry Brown, Poole's chief modeller after the departure of W. C. Unwin.[9] These first two designs were added to in the following years with a series of sailing boats, shells and other marine subjects appropriate to Poole's location. In addition Poole also produced their own version of the three-part flying duck ornament so much denigrated in more recent times but so overwhelmingly popular during the 1930s and after the Second World

Part of a teaset, Streamline shape, designed by John Adams, the decoration designed by Truda Carter and painted by Ruth Pavely. *c.* 1936–7. *Victoria & Albert Museum.*

Part of a coffee set, Studland shape, designed by Harold Stabler, produced in plain glazes including Sapphire Blue and, in this case, Apple Green. An equivalent shape in teaware was also made. *c.* 1930–33. *Victoria & Albert Museum.*

Dish, *Waterwitch*, designed by Arthur Bradbury and painted by Margaret Holder in blue, yellow and black. 1932. *Private collection.*

War. A special Poole range of flying seagulls was also made, and while the Pottery was undoubtedly playing to the lower end of the popular market, their ducks and seagulls were well made and particularly well glazed in sprayed colours of some subtlety.

As with the painted designs, various friends and art school contacts also contributed to the figure range. One such was Harold Brownsword, who was a close friend of John Adams' from Royal College days and who had produced designs for the figure side of the Pottery's production from the early 1920s for about ten years. He is known to have been responsible for a modelled book-end in the form of an elephant leaning forward standing among leaves, designed between 1921 and 1925; a square honey box and cover surmounted with a bee, which was issued with both plain glazes and also with painted colours and the ubiquitous spot edge; also, a figure of a knight on horseback, a mantlepiece ornament which was designed around 1930.[10]

Pair of doves with vines, designed by John Adams, modelled by Harry Brown and glazed in blues and greens, an adaptation of a bookend introduced in about 1930. *c.* 1935. *Victoria & Albert Museum.*

Other novelties were attempted. Shortly before the Second World War the Pottery made stoneware garden labels, stencilled with the names of popular plants. These were launched at the Chelsea Flower Show but, unfortunately, they were not taken up by the public.[11] While Poole continued to exhibit at the usual trade fairs they also contributed to various specialist and more prestigious shows. The first of these exhibitions was held at Dorland Hall in Regent Street by the British Institute of Industrial Art in 1933 and was entitled British Industrial Art in Relation to the Home. Since its inception in 1919, the B.I.I.A. had been pursuing its primary object, 'to raise the standard of modern British industrial art, and at the same time to stimulate public appreciation of works of industrial art, so as to increase the volume and raise the quality of the demand for those works.'[12] The B.I.I.A. was loaned the North Court in the Victoria and Albert Museum in which to house its growing permanent collections and also to provide accommodation for the Institute's annual exhibition. In addition to these yearly activities the B.I.I.A. was consulted in connection with many other exhibitions, some international, as well as mounting its own major shows in this country, such as the Dorland Hall event. The 1933 exhibition was of special significance, being the first in that decade of a series of important opportunities for manufacturers to demonstrate their technical and design advances. C.S.A. grasped the chance to show Picotee ware in both decorative and dinner set form. Also included in their selection were a large number of stoneware pieces catalogued as designed by John Adams, Truda Carter and Harold Stabler collectively, and two of the large dishes decorated with Arthur Bradbury's sailing ships, *Poole Whaler* and *Waterwitch*.[13]

Two years later, in 1935, an exhibition, English Pottery Old and New, was held at the Victoria and Albert Museum. Although small, it attracted favourable notice in the more discerning journals. It was mounted jointly by the Museum and the Council for Art and Industry. The C.A.I., the third organization of importance in promoting twentieth-century industrial and handicraft design, was formed in 1934 following a report commissioned by the Board of Trade from a committee headed by Lord Gorell. Frank Pick, influential vice-chairman of London Passenger Transport Board, and long-term acquaintance of Cyril Carter and Harold Stabler, was appointed chairman of the Council and devoted the last seven

years of his life to it. His contact with Cyril and Stabler stemmed
not only from their membership of the D.I.A. and the B.I.I.A. but
also the Tileworks' involvement with the new London Underground stations. Part of the Council's established programme was
for a series of exhibitions to be held at the Victoria and Albert
Museum and for acquisitions to be made from these displays for
the Museum's collections. At the same time items lent to the
Council by manufacturers were shown outside London through
the existing travelling exhibition service run by the Museum's
Circulation Department. English Pottery Old and New was the
second of these shows (the first was of silver work, in 1934), and
was so successful that an illustrated souvenir was issued the following year; its cover was designed by the distinguished graphic
artist, Edward McKnight Kauffer. In the exhibition contemporary
wares were selected for their qualities of sound design and satisfying appearance, under the best Design and Industries Association principles. Selection was made by the Museum's senior
ceramic specialists, W. B. Honey and Bernard Rackham (of whom
John Adams had such pleasant student memories) with a committee which also included Harry Trethowan. The wares were
shown in comparison with their historical precedents in design and
technique. John Adams arranged for the dispatch of a range of
C.S.A. production – tableware, painted decorative pieces and some
stonewares – and as a result of this exhibition examples of designs
by Truda Carter, John Adams and Harry Trethowan were
acquired for the Museum's collections.

Also in 1935, another exhibition was held, this time at the Royal
Academy. It was arranged by the Royal Society of Arts itself, a
new venture for a normally cautious body which had not previously
encountered the industrial world in this way. The ceramics selection committee consisted of Joseph Burton, Cyril Carter, W. Reid
Dick, Gordon Forsyth, A. E. Gray, C. Geoffrey Holme, Ernest
Johnson, C. J. Noke, Harry Trethowan, J. T. Webster and Josiah
Wedgwood, many of them the senior representatives of the pottery
industry. C.S.A. exhibited John Adams' stoneware with Mirror
Black, rhododendron ash, iron brown, Autumn Brown and various
other glazes simply described as 'high temperature'. Truda
Carter's painted designs were also shown in company with pots
designed by Harry Trethowan and Harold Stabler glazed with the
production colours Magnolia White, Korean Green and Old Ivory.

Pierced tray, designed by John Adams and sprayed with Picotee glazes in browns.
c. 1935. *Private collection. Photograph: Victoria & Albert Museum.*

All these pieces were for sale and the stoneware varied in price
from 15s. to £7.[14]

However, the major event of the decade, as it had been twelve
years earlier, was the International Exhibition held in Paris in
1937. The selection of pieces for this exhibition was made by the
Council for Art and Industry. Each section was put under an
individual selection committee appointed by the Council and that
for pottery and glass consisted of F. V. Burridge, Cyril Carter, W.
B. Dalton, Gordon Forsyth, W. B. Honey, Geoffrey Pilkington and
Josiah Wedgwood, many of them by then experienced in this type

Part of the exhibition 'English Pottery Old and New', Victoria & Albert Museum, 1935. Left: *hors d'oeuvre* set, the pattern designed by Truda Carter, the shape probably designed by John Adams, and painted by Ruth Pavely. *c.* 1934–5. Right: three dishes probably designed by Harold Stabler, with a Magnolia White glaze. *c* 1934–5. *Victoria & Albert Museum.*

Part of the exhibition 'English Pottery Old & New', Victoria & Albert Museum, 1935. Left: vase designed by Harry Trethowan with a Polar White glaze. Centre: bowl designed by John Adams with a Magnolia White glaze. *Victoria & Albert Museum.* Right: vase possibly designed by John Adams. *c.* 1934–5. Whereabouts unknown. *Photograph: Victoria & Albert Museum.*

of exhibition work. C.S.A. exhibited a range of wares consisting of an *hors d'oeuvre* set and dinner set with painted decoration; a coffee set, Studland shape with Apple Green glaze and a white dinner service by Harold Stabler; a white coffee set by John Adams; and white celadon and ivory bowls and vases by Adams and Truda. In the introduction to this section W. B. Honey wrote

As far as the best work of the factories is concerned in this matter of Chinese influence we may say that to a beautiful simplicity and fitness of form is now added a notable charm of glaze quality. Foremost perhaps in this new field were the firm of Carter, Stabler and Adams, with a range of fine cream, white and smoky-brown glazes, applied to forms which owe something to Far Eastern influence.[15]

As the 1930s drew to a close the Pottery had gained an enviable reputation, in the eyes of contemporary observers, for distinctive and distinguished wares. C.S.A. was always among the first few potteries chosen to represent British production in company with well-established giants such as Wedgwood, Copeland and Doulton. On the selling side, after many lean years spent in striving towards a specialized objective set by its artistic partners, particularly John Adams, commercial success was on the horizon in the form of sound tableware design and greatly improved standardized glazes.

6
1921-1930

Carter & Co., the Tileworks: the Stablers, memorials and individual tile designs

W H I L E the Pottery was establishing a separate identity and acquiring a significant reputation, the Tileworks were recovering from the effects of the war shortages, regaining and building upon the status they had enjoyed in pre-war years. In 1917 Carter & Co. took an entire stand at the British Industries Fair held at the Victoria and Albert Museum and the Imperial Institute at South Kensington. They showed, in company with some unspecified 'Art Pottery', a selection of their production and were entered in the catalogue as:

Manufacturers of Floor Tiles in plain colours, vitreous and encaustic, Enamelled Tiles in all colours. Handmade Anglo-Dutch Glazed tiles; Leadless Glazed Tiles; White Glazed Tiles; Glazed Cappings, Skirtings, Angles and Coves of all descriptions. Ceramic Mosaic in fan-shape, squares, hexagons and circles. Marble Mosaic, Terrazzo, Fireplaces and Fenders in Glazed and Unglazed Tiles, Briquettes and Faience. Constructional Ceramic Material in Terra Cotta, Ceramic Marble and Faience.[1]

It is very doubtful that they would have been able to fulfil many orders from this range at that time – the manufacture of much of it was forbidden in 1917 anyway – but by the early 1920s they were well on the return to full production.

The arrival of Harold and Phoebe Stabler made a great impact on the Tileworks' output. Their particular influence was on the faience department, and one of the most important commissions in the inter-war period was that for a war memorial for Durban, South Africa, which was completed in 1925. The entire group consisted of a Christ figure supported between two elaborately winged angels beneath an irradiating sun over 20ft high. Nothing quite like it had been attempted before at Poole. The 14 tons of clay had to be erected hollow and without an armature, the relief projected to a depth of 17 in. and it had to be kept in position for four months after it had been made, to allow for gradual and controlled drying. The memorial was built at the East Quay works and to accommodate the great height the first floor was completely removed. A sloping easel was constructed with ledges at intervals to support the clay mass, and the back was made in such a way that sections could be removed in order to check the back of the enormous clay slab and to keep it moist. The shrinkage in the foot of clay was $^{11}/_{16}$ in. and this too had to be taken into consideration. It was fired in sections weighing about 2 cwt.[2] Because it was such a major production, stories about this memorial abound, the most often repeated one being that of the glaze firing. When the sections including the angels' heads were taken from the glost kiln, it was found that the application of glazes to the eyes and faces had been reversed, and consequently their faces were blue and their eyes white (in the raw state the difference between the two glaze colours is difficult to distinguish). Fortunately the offending colours were successfully chipped off, the sections re-glazed and re-fired correctly.

As far as anyone can remember, very few people at Poole seem to have been involved in modelling or making the memorial, beyond the technical aspects. Harry Brown, Poole's chief modeller, may have helped, and someone was employed to care for the clay – spraying it to keep it moist in Stabler's absence. Ernest Castle, who worked with tile samples and as a typist, was used as a model for the Christ figure.[3] When it was finished the sections were assembled in order on the Pottery floor and numbered. Margaret Holder made a tracing and indicated the jointing.[4] A week before it was due for shipping, Carter's employees were allowed to bring in their families to view this enormous achievement.[5]

In January 1925 the *Pottery Gazette and Glass Trade Review* printed the following:

It is seldom that a work of such dimensions and technical interest is done in glazed faience. The whole memorial, from ground to the top, is 56 ft., and the Della Robbia work commences 24 ft. above the ground level, so that it calls for a very formal and clear-cut modelling, so as to take its place in the architectural scheme and to be quite 'readable' at such a height. The glazed sculpture is 21ft. high and 11ft. across. Some idea of

Harold Stabler at work on the Durban War Memorial. 1925. *Pilkington Tiles Ltd.*

the magnitude of the work will be gained when it is said that the angels are 12ft. in height, and that 14 tons of clay were used in the group.

The colouring is in the traditional white, blue, yellow, orange, and green of the Italian Della Robbias, these colours being heightened with gold on the haloes of the angels and the sun. Such bright colour has an entirely different value in the brilliant sunlight of South Africa than it would have in the comparatively cold light in this country, as the sun takes any suggestion of crudeness out of it, and seems to purify the colour until it looks as fresh and clean as a watercolour drawing.

A recumbent effigy of a South African soldier lies in state underneath this coloured sculpture, which represents the spirit of the soldier being taken up by the two angels. Bronze panels at the sides record the names in inlaid enamels of 1,000 Durban men who made the great sacrifice, while a great bronze candelabra is fixed in front of the coloured group, with a light that will always be burning. It will thus be realised that the effect at night will be extraordinarily suggestive and poetic.

The last pieces of the work were landed at Durban during November, and the unveiling of the memorial should not now be long delayed.[6]

In 1927, a Professor Oxley of Durban was reported to have 'seen the Durban memorial since it had been erected, and was much impressed with it. The whole of the glazed ware had arrived without any damage whatever. It was particularly suitable to the sunny climate of South Africa, where pigments were liable to fade'.[7]

While this was the major achievement of the 1920s, work was also completed on other projects. The Durban memorial was, in fact, the Stablers' second monument. In 1922 they executed a similar commission for Rugby School consisting of a central figure of St George seated on a dapple-grey horse astride a fallen dragon, and flanked on either side by standing figures holding swags of flowers and garlands. This was worked on by both husband and wife – Harold modelling St George and Phoebe the supporting figures. As with the Durban memorial it is possible that Harry Brown helped with this, probably on the modelling of the swags and garlands. Margaret Holder's first lettering job was to paint the names on the memorial, finishing the work on Good Friday 1922.[8] The memorial was constructed to stand above a fireplace and is therefore on a much smaller scale than the Durban work, the St George figure standing no more than 3 ft 6 in. high.[9]

At least one spare set of casts was made and portions were shown extensively in the 1920s in exhibitions. The first was held by the British Institute of Industrial Art in the Victoria and Albert Museum in 1922. A section was included in the British Empire Exhibition held at Wembley in 1924 and also in the International Exhibition of Modern Decorative and Industrial Art in Paris in 1925. It was also illustrated widely in contemporary journals.

Having established this type of faience sculpture as their especial contribution to the works' output, Harold and Phoebe Stabler continued to make architectural features in this style throughout the 1920s. In about 1926 they jointly modelled a group of decorative panels for the mortuary at the Kensington Infirmary. In addition to such commissions, they also produced a number of

The Rugby School War Memorial. *Architectural Review, 1922.*

'Shy', garden figure designed
by Phoebe Stabler, with
mottled buff glaze. 1914–22.
Victoria & Albert Museum.

'Harpy Eagle', garden figure
designed by Harold Stabler,
with brown and black glazes.
Produced and exhibited by
Carter & Co. throughout the
1920s. 1916. *Victoria & Albert
Museum.*

smaller figures and panels intended for garden use. These ranged from an eagle perched on a rock, 'The Harpy Eagle', modelled by Harold Stabler, which stood about 2 ft in height, to fauns and cherubic children in various guises which were Phoebe's speciality. While these figures usually merited a separate advertisement under the heading 'Garden Statuary', some of the smallest were marketed through the pottery catalogues in company with the domestic, ornamental figures which were largely Phoebe's province. One exception to this appears to be 'The Bull', which is signed by both partners and dated 1914. From 1921 these figures were made and sold through the catalogues, although their production falls some-where between the Pottery and the Tileworks. The smaller figures were, initially, press-moulded and later slip-cast, in a buff-coloured body, fired at near stoneware temperature. The exact date that slip casting for these figures became normal practice is not definite, but it is probably some time in the mid-1920s. Pamela Diamand, who accompanied her father Roger Fry on a weekend's potting at Poole, distinctly remembers seeing large slip-cast figures for dairies and butchers' shops, although none of them seems to have sur-vived.[10] These, then, would have been cast in the same way as the moulded architectural sections. Apparently slip casting for the smaller pieces was not introduced until much later. Other panels, plaques or models, mostly by Harold Stabler, were made in rough, light red faience ware, and despite their architectural purposes were fired at Poole. These included smaller relief panels and the famous galleon which was adopted as an unofficial symbol of the Pottery and featured in the catalogues. Smaller versions of this were subsequently developed by Harry Brown.[11]

For building facing and constructional work, the most commonly employed architectural ware was Carter's Ceramic Marble, devel-oped in about 1909 by Alfred Eason (who received £10 from the profits on Ceramic Marble in that year) to compete with the similar material made by rival firms, such as Doulton's Carrara.[12] Ceramic Marble was made in a warm, creamy-white, slightly speckled; a clearer white; and blues and greens. Its particular property was that it was craze-proof and therefore highly resistant to seawater and weather. This was a special advantage to a tile-works based on the coast who could boast firsthand knowledge of the problems of seaside towns and thus gain contracts for band-stands, piers, colonnades and all the types of architecture exclusive to coastal resorts. These claims also held good for inland city atmospheres. The material was unusual in that it was fired only once, the glaze being applied to the 'green' body and the biscuit and glost firing combined in one and at a higher temperature than normal.

In about 1920 a small construction in the form of a Greek temple was put up at one of the trade fairs to demonstrate the remarkable properties of Ceramic Marble. A column was ostentatiously smothered with red ink by James Radley Young, and then with theatrical nonchalance he sauntered off, leaving the dye to do its worst and sink, revealingly, into any cracks or crazing. On his return he wiped the column clean with a flourish.[13] Ceramic Marble was used in commissions such as the bandstand and colonnade at Eastbourne, the pier frontage at Hastings, Plummer's and Bright's stores in Bournemouth (the latter now under the name of Dingle's) and numerous public houses, hotels and cinemas along the south coast and inland.

As with the Pottery, there was an influx of new staff to the Tileworks around 1920. The mosaic department, another Carter speciality, increased in size. In 1920 it was under the charge of Alfred Onslow, and the main work then was flooring for grocery shops such as Lipton's, the Co-operative and International stores. The assembly of the mosaic patterns was done by girls and in 1920 the method was still as it had been before the First World War. The girls chopped up the mosaic manually on a 3-in. square, thick piece of lead which they held on their laps. Owen Carter described the method in 1893:

These floors are all worked [out] on paper stretched on boards. The actual size of the space to be filled having been drawn thereon, the tesserae are affixed face downwards to the paper by means of gum. [Onslow made up his own water-soluble recipe which included black treacle.] As soon as the required area is finished, and the gum dry, it is broken into pieces of convenient sizes for packing. When the floor has to be laid, these fragments of mosaic, with the paper upwards, are placed, fitting one into the other, on to a previously prepared cement bed. When all is in position, water is thrown over it, which, added to the moisture from the cement, softens the gum, so that the paper is easily removed, and the surface of the floor seen for the first time.[14]

The building where these patterns were made and assembled was

Eastbourne, Grand Parade extension, showing the use of Ceramic Marble. *c.* 1930.
Pilkington Tiles Ltd.

known as the Mosaic Building and was situated on the northern
side of East Quay Road. It was originally a fish warehouse built
during the time of the cod trade with Newfoundland, for which
Poole was the major British port, and the building was demolished
in 1972.

While the mosaic department provided decorative flooring, the
design department, also at East Quay and headed by James Radley
Young, continued to produce painted panels. The faience department was, by this time, under the charge of Bill Eason and in this
last decade of his life J. R. Y. concentrated almost entirely on tile

CARTER TILES
POOLE   LONDON

painting. Young's right-hand man at this point was Arthur Nickols, who joined the firm in about 1920 and who specialized in the smaller roundels and plaques. Where J. R. Y. painted the complete pastoral scene – fields, trees and cattle – it was Nickols who painted portrait heads of individual cows or bulls.[15] He had no previous training, and like all other unqualified trainees he went to evening classes at the local art schools. The studies for his work were further extended during the day with bicycling trips into the surrounding countryside where he would find and sketch any suitable animals.[16] As befitted the senior and junior artist, Radley Young generally signed his work in monogram, while Nickols' art appeared unattributed (G. B. Tull's butcher's shop in Wickham, near Portsmouth, is an example).[17] Nickols designed at least one set of wall tiles for the Tileworks. These were twelve painted designs of fish and are shown in a tile catalogue of about 1939. Although Nickols' work was almost entirely on the painted panels he probably also did some lettering. In the late 1920s and early 1930s Poole made some faience grave edgings and headstones in the form of 'open books'. These were probably modelled by Harry Brown and lettered by Nickols; there are a number in Poole Cemetery. This is not the only instance of the Pottery's involvement in funerary work. Harry Brown and Margaret Holder made and lettered cremation urns for Toc H, which were still being made when Miss Holder left in 1941.[18] One further piece of Nickols' design work was the symbol of the dolphin leaping in a curve over a bottle kiln which, like the Stabler galleon, was adopted as an unofficial trade mark and which is still shown at the wall-tile works today.

While the scenic panels were painted in this way, at the White Works, where wall tiles were produced in quantity, individual tile designs were painted and stencilled by a small team of three or four people in the hand-painting department. Here various methods were in use. Designs could be painted on to a fired, matt-glazed tile, a thin coat of the same matt glaze was then applied over, allowed to dry and then brushed with a coat of turpentine before the final firing. A second method was to paint on the

Carter & Co. stand at the Building Trades Exhibition, 1928, showing the Harold Stabler galleon and a mosaic floor design adapted from a Stabler faience panel. *Pilkington Tiles Ltd.*

completely unglazed biscuit and then to spray a clear glaze over. Alternatively, stencilled decoration which incorporated a painted outline was applied to tiles which were glazed with a pot facing, fired and then infilled with painting. Again a thin coat of the same matt glaze was applied over, allowed to dry and then brushed over with a mixture of Canada Balsam and turpentine. The tile was then stencilled and fired.[19] All three methods involved the use of colours made from metallic oxides mixed with water, and all three seem to have been in use at the same time. The finished effect looked much the same as the painted pottery. All the methods were of the in-glaze technique, and the same semi-matt glaze was used at both the Pottery and the Tileworks.

Once again Harold Stabler not only designed his own range of

Group of three tiles, Farmyard series, designed by E. E. Stickland. *c.* 1925. *Victoria & Albert Museum.*

tiles, Waterbirds, but also brought with him designers from the Royal College. Some, like Edward Bawden, were still students. About 1922 Bawden designed a series of tiles based on the related subjects The Chase and Sporting which were produced during the 1920s as painted decoration. In the 1930s these two subjects were still made but with slight variations and were even continued after the war in a much altered form. Although Bawden had long wished them to be discontinued they formed a lastingly popular subject. In addition to these designs actually made by Bawden, a tile panel was produced based on his frontispiece to the booklet *Pottery Making at Poole*, published in about 1922 and mentioned earlier. The adaptation was made by Margaret Holder who painted two ver-

'The House of Tiles', Carter & Co. stand at the Ideal Homes Exhibition in 1927, showing tiles and faience designed by Phoebe Stabler (the roundel) and Reginald Till (the wall, floor tiles and faience screen). *Pilkington Tiles Ltd.*

'Piping Faun' roundel, designed by Phoebe Stabler, screen and column, designed by Reginald Till, and urn, possibly designed by Harold Stabler. All, with the exception of the roundel, are from the Ideal Homes Exhibition stand of 1927 and are here incorporated into John Adams' house 'Stellawood', at Broadstone.
Photograph: Pilkington Tiles Ltd.

sions, one for the Pottery and one for Poole bus station, into which she introduced a bus.[20] Unfortunately this second version no longer survives.

In addition to the mosaic floors made for food stores, wall tiles were also produced with suitable decoration. E. E. Stickland, who had started at Carter & Co. before 1921,[21] designed a series of such tiles entitled Farmyard. This handsome set included a turkey, chickens, ducks, geese, rabbits, sheep, pigs, a goat, a Shire horse, a windmill and a haystack. They were made in both painted and stencilled versions from about 1922. These tiles were used by Dewhursts and Mac Fisheries, among others. In about 1925 the latter firm commissioned at least seven marine designs for use on their fish paste lids and packaging labels, as a sales promotion idea intended to attract the pot lid collector. They observed that, 'Pot-lid collecting has been a fashion now for many years, very large sums being paid for certain of the original ideas. . . . As the sketches . . . are all the work of first class artists, it is anticipated that the public will find an additional inducement in collecting the complete range.'[22] The first seven designs were Fishing Smacks, The Fisher Girl, On the Wings of the Wind, Seagull, Galleon, Caller Herrin', Royal Sturgeon, and an eighth was based on the Mac Fisheries Four Fish symbol. Three of these designs were applied to tiles by Carter & Co. for Mac Fisheries' use, while the pot lids were made by another, unidentified, firm. Dora M. Batty designed a herring girl with a basket of fish on her head (Caller Herrin'); Minnie McLeish a sunset scene with boats (Fishing Smacks); and Irene Fawkes probably designed a seagull flying low above waves (Seagull).[23] This last tile design is exceptional in that it differs from the pot lid version considerably.

Another popular range of tiles were those designed by Joseph Roelants. After his arrival in Poole from Belgium he designed a series which was issued in two different colourways, known as Blue Dutch and Coloured Dutch. At the 1917 British Industries Fair, Carter & Co. advertised 'Anglo-Dutch Glazed Tiles'. There are no further details in the catalogue and this description may simply refer to the tin-glaze coating. However, Roelants' designs were certainly produced on hand-painted tiles before 1920 and possibly some were already made and shown in 1917. As the range name suggests, the series was based on rural, village and seashore scenes of Belgium and Holland. They were reproduced either in colours or in blue on a white ground and were made in both hand-painted or stencilled versions. Their popularity meant that, like the Farmyard series, they stayed in production until about 1939.

It is worth emphasizing at this point the great sense of 'family' felt by those who worked at Carter's. Obviously there were problems and grievances about pay, status and recognition, particularly among those who reached the more managerial levels. But among the ordinary employees there was a great feeling of comradeship sustained by the annual outings and Christmas parties, which were established back in the 1880s and 1890s. The community sense was further developed not only by the continuation of these activities after the First World War but also by the great expectations put upon the staff, particularly the artistic and design sections. Despite the poor working conditions there was great competition for work at Poole and Hamworthy. Undoubtedly much of this was the result of the employment problems of the time, but even so, for artistically inclined school-leavers or ex-students with an art, architectural or chemistry training, the potteries were attractive. Everyone was expected to attend the local art schools where many of Carter's staff taught – Unwin, Young, Eason, Gertie Gilham and Reginald Till among them. Leslie Coombe attended evening classes five times a week for instance, with others, and Carter's paid the fees even though he had already had some training at Derby School of Art.[24] Those already trained or qualified brought portfolios of work to their interview.

These extra activities outside working hours, from Christmas parties to evening study, are now recalled with great affection by those involved. Carter's Christmas celebrations were held at the Antelope Hotel in Poole, where art school fancy dress parties were also held.[25] These appear to have been very lively occasions where even the normally unsmiling managing director, Benjamin Elford, was persuaded to relax. Cyril, of course, was in his element enjoying these celebrations and also the times when he invited parties to his own home, 'Yaffle Hill', during the 1930s. Some idea of the jollity is given by the 'Karters' Kommunity Karols', written by 'Karters' Keramic Kommunity Khoir' and sung to popular tunes.

No. 1. (*There is a Tavern in the Town*)
(Dedicated to the Regular Diners)

There is a Buffet in this Town, in this Town,
    Where we of Carter's Staff sit down, all sit down,
And take our lunch, 'mid laughter light and free,
    And at four o'clock we take our tea.

Chorus:–
Fare-thee-well my work, I leave thee,
    Do not let my parting grieve thee,
For remember that the best of friends must part, must part,
    I go, to chew, dear friend, to chew, to chew, to chew,

The Beef Steak and the Irish Stew, Irish Stew,
    Baked Potatoes and the nimble Pea,
And may this grub go well with me.
We all roll up at one o'clock, one o'clock,
    And Nippy in her neat black frock, neat black frock,
Dishes up the 'eats', 'mid laughter light and free,
    Oh, may the Beef go well with me.

Chorus:–
Fare-thee-well, etc.

The menu varies day by day, day by day,
    From tripe and onions to 'souflay', to 'souflay',
And we masticate, 'mid laughter light and free,
    Oh, may the juice go well with me.

Chorus:–
Fare-thee-well etc.

And now, I think we'll all agree, all agree,
    The shilling spent by you and me, you and me,
Fills us with cheer, and laughter light and free,
    And makes the world go well with we.

Chorus:–
Fare-thee-well, etc.

No. 2 (*John Brown's Body*)

Carter's Crackle Glazes, have a Curious Kind of Craze,
Carter's Crackle Glazes, have a Curious Kind of Craze,
Carter's Crackle Glazes, have a Curious Kind of Craze,
And this Curious Kind of Crazy Crackle's Carter's Crackle Glaze.

Chorus:–
When the body's Anglo Tiquew,
When the body's Anglo Tiquew,
When the body's Anglo Tiquew,
This Curious Kind of Crazy Crackling Glaze goes Crackling on.

No. 3 (*Three Blind Mice*)
(Dedicated to the Tea Swillers)

Four o'clock; Four o'clock; Four o'clock;
See how they run; see how they run; see how they run;
They all run up for their cup of tea,
That's served for them by the fair Nippy,
Did you ever see such industry,
At Four o'clock.

No. 4 (*Good King Wenceslas*)

Carter's Offices look out,
    On the roofs of houses,
Where the clothes hang round about,
    Shirts and Pants and Trousers,
Petticoats and wet Chemise,
    Stockings in abundance,
What an inspiration these,
    To our correspundance. [sic]

We have Central Heating too,
    And it often stays there,
People in the middle stew,
    While the others freeze there,
Smells of drying overcoats,
    On the radiators,
Mingle with the Cookhouse groats
    And the baked potatoes.

Life at Carter's can't be tame
    With such entertainments,
And we really aren't to blame,
    For our poor attainments,
Really things might be much worse,
    Than they are at present,
Being businesslike and terse,
    Isn't very pleasant.

7
1930-1939

Carter & Co., the Tileworks:
major contracts and exhibitions

W H I L E Harold Stabler was the mainstay of the decorative faience department production, he was also responsible for the introduction of Reginald Till to the Tileworks, in 1923. Like so many of Stabler's contacts, Till was an ex-Royal College of Art student. He had followed his studies with a travelling scholarship to Scandinavia. In going north he suppressed his personal and particular passion which was for Della Robbia faience; his first choice had been Italy, naturally. However, in 1922, with a career to think of, Sweden was in the forefront of the type of architecture which Till expected to be his life's work and so he went to study municipal architecture and housing.[1] But it was his interest in Della Robbia that attracted Stabler's attention. Till began working at East Quay, Poole, on the faience side but later also worked at the wall and floor tile departments at Hamworthy.

In 1927 Till first made a major impression. That year he prepared an Ideal Home Exhibition stand for Carter's which caught the attention of the Cunard architect for the *Queen Mary*, the prestige luxury liner then under construction. Till's previous exhibition experience was in the design of a pottery roundel (no more detailed description given) shown in the International Exhibition of Modern Decorative and Industrial Art in Paris in 1925.[2] He and James Radley Young had visited that exhibition and, influenced by what he had seen, Till designed for Carter's Ideal Home stand a handsome pierced screen of scrolls and curlicues, unmistakably in the French manner and therefore very contemporary and stylish. The screen, modelled by Harry Brown, was supported at one end by a fluted column surmounted by an urn filled with thick, chunky flowers. The urn was not by Till and may have been designed by Harold Stabler; it is similar in style to other designs of flower-filled urns for relief plaques known to have been by Stabler. Phoebe Stabler's roundels, including the one known as 'The Piping Faun', were set into the walls, but the decorative tiling and the large urn on the floor were to Till's designs. Soon after this exhibition an invitation was received from Cunard for a design for the first-class swimming pool. At this point, of course, James Radley Young was still chief designer (he died soon after, in 1933) and it was a classic case of the senior man fulfilling the commission which had been intended for the junior. Cunard returned Radley Young's drawings indicating that they had expected something in the style of the exhibition stand. Till produced a sumptuous design[3] and he and Leslie Coombe went up to Brown's shipyard to make the detailed drawings. The work was considerably advanced before financial problems forced Cunard to cut back and Till's obviously expensive scheme, with its turquoise and gold colouring and individual modelling, was axed. In its place he made a far more utilitarian scheme, less extravagant and continental, more cautious and, of necessity, based on mass production methods and Carter's own standard ware. Nevertheless he was able to introduce some touches of individuality, particularly with the flooring. This was decorated with tubeline patterns and was therefore attractive while the raised decoration provided an effectively non-slip surface. In the end, the *Queen Mary* commission became more of a considerable technical achievement than a design triumph. There were major problems with the conflicting curves on the ship and the overhead blocks were eventually fixed in place on runners rolled in from each end and, in effect, hung like curtains. Much of this work was done by Bill Eason and Billy Bryant, resolving the conflicts between cornice angles and the rhomboid section of the hull, before passing the full-size drawings on to the plaster shop to make the moulds.[4] Not only did the main ceramic faience sections have to be fitted in this way, but the curve problems also affected the tiling. The wall tiling in the bathrooms also had to be rhomboid, curving in two directions.[5]

Despite this setback Till's contribution to the design of tiles was extensive. His use of tubelining updated a technique hitherto associated mainly with the *Art Nouveau* designs of twenty years earlier. In 1930 he designed another stand for Carter's, this time

The entrance to 'Yaffle Hill', showing the faience woodpecker above the doorway, drawn out by Bill Eason. *Pilkington Tiles Ltd.*

for the Building Trades Exhibition, in which he demonstrated the possibilities of this method of decoration with a striking and lively setting in Islamic style. Here he returned to another great passion of his student days. He employed, with great verve, the character-istically vivid blues and pinks in a geometric pattern enriched with stylized flower forms reminiscent of ancient Egyptian designs based on the papyrus plant motif. The panels were subsequently built into the showroom walls at East Quay and may still be seen on the staircase entrance to the craft section. He also experimented with the technique of spraying designs through stencils (spraying was first introduced at Carter's in 1919 or 1920) and one of these experimental patterns was later developed by Truda Carter into the zig-zag frieze used in the C.S.A. tea-rooms.

When Cyril Carter and Truda Adams married in about 1931 they moved into a new house, 'Yaffle Hill'; the architect was Sir Edward Maufe. John Gloag, the important critic and observer of twentieth-century design, described it in *The Architect and Building News* in January 1932. He pictured the outside in lyrical terms:

Built on the shoulder of a hill, it is a house of varying levels, in plan like the spread wings of a gliding bird, with the axial line of the bird's body running due north and south. The tall arcaded windows of a big room and a study, and the slender bay of the dining-room look southward and frame a connected picture of a lawn with a stone-lipped pool, and beyond the land falls away in tiers of pinewoods to Poole and its harbour, and beyond, again, are the Purbeck hills, with the gaunt tooth of Corfe Castle visible where the hills open. A broad paved walk of Purbeck stone sep-arates these windows from the lawn. Externally the house, standing alone and back by trees, wears white and blue: smooth white walls ascending to a roof of Chinese-blue glazed pantiles, from which twin chimney-stacks arise. The metal-framed windows echo the colour of the pantiles. A course of oyster-grey moulded faience runs along the parapet of the balconies that open out of the east and west bedrooms, and this grey band becomes the sill line of the southward windows of the upper storey. The architraves of the arched windows on the ground floor are of the same grey faience.

. . . The welcome begins at the entrance, where a balcony projects over the porch, flashing from its centre like an heraldic emblem a 'yaffle'

Group of tiles, designed by Harold Stabler, for the London Underground, commissioned by Frank Pick, vice-chairman of London Passenger Transport Board. *c.* 1938–9. *London Transport Museum.*

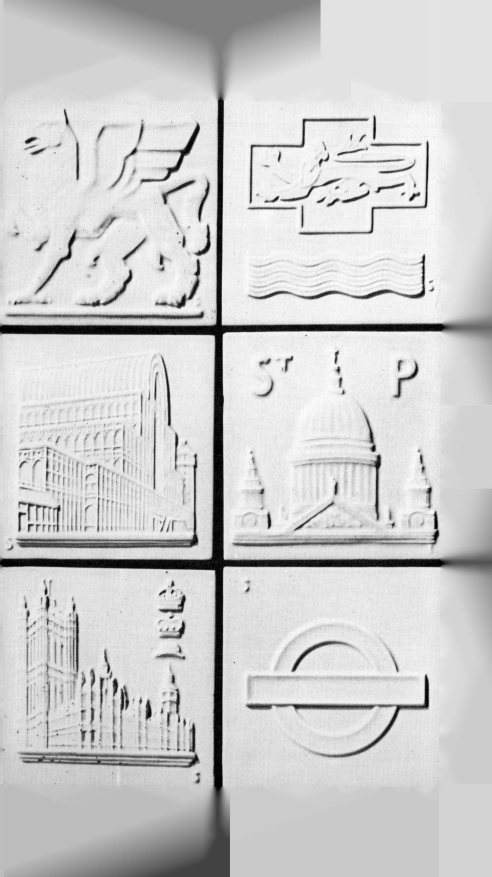

Illustration from Carter & Co. (Tiles) brochure of a tile panel for the children's ward, King Edward Hospital, Ealing, showing Princesses Elizabeth and Margaret Rose, designer unknown. 1935. *Phyllis Butler.*

(woodpecker) in coloured faience, its beak pickaxing at the bark of a tree – an appropriate embellishment. The entrance sheltered by the balcony has a broad architrave of black faience, presenting four surfaces that are stepped back towards the doorway, one of them enriched with a wave of moulding. The doors themselves consist of two sheets of opaque glass set in metal frames, each guarded by a simple iron grille in Chinese blue. On the floor of the entrance hall is a mosaic replica of the house, an amusing piece of decorative shorthand, that includes the Carter potteries (which can be seen from the house down by the harbour), and the initials of the owner and architect. . . .

The Carter potteries were of course deeply involved with the construction of 'Yaffle Hill'. The 'simple iron grilles in Chinese blue' were closely based on Reginald Till's pierced screen of 1927, and it is possible that Cyril would have used the original in some way if John Adams had not already appropriated it to adorn his own house at Broadstone, 'Stellawood'. Bill Eason drew out the faience coping and this, the blue pantiles and the faience woodpecker were specially made and fired at Carter's. The mosaic floor to the entrance hall was the work of Alfred Onslow and his team. Much of the general flooring and wall tiles were provided by Carter's and a subsidiary company, Art Pavements and Decorations Ltd, was also employed.

Gloag completed his description with yet more praise:

A few surfaces, restricted in area, are enlivened with vivid colour. The bathrooms upstairs are polished fantasies. In one, grey, white, black and vermilion do themselves honour in a geometric but imaginative mosaic pattern, and in the bathroom that is part of the west bedroom suite, where mellow greens are restfully associated, there are grey and pale green tiles, punctuated by a few tiles enriched with a wave moulding in dark silver. Soft pink walls and grey paint in the east bedroom; soft red doors with mauve-grey architraves in the bedroom corridor. Everywhere there has been an attempt to weld rooms into companiable unities, and everywhere the attempt has succeeded. . . .[6]

No wonder the Carters were so proud of the house and no wonder that the employees who visited it in those early days were so astonished.

The 1930s were a time of great achievement for Carter & Co. They worked on the most prestigious contracts for buildings in the forefront of modern design – the Firestone factory, the Hoover factory and the De La Warr Pavilion at Bexhill.

The first part of the Firestone factory, on the Great West Road through Brentford, in Middlesex, was completed early in 1929 and was an important landmark in architectural design. The architects were Wallis, Gilbert & Partners and the building is one of the impressive pre-war industrial buildings which march down either side of the freeway, each an individual architectural entity and yet united into a cross between the imposing vista of the Washington Smithsonian mall and a conveniently space-saving estate of Hollywood epic sets. The central Firestone office block, facing the road, was reviewed in the *Architectural Journal*:

Externally, the finish of what is as yet only the central portion of a facade which will eventually mask the working premises in their rear, is in white cement, except for the main piers, which are faced in stone. A striking decorative scheme is obtained by the insertion of tiles of decided but harmonious colours to mark the main entrance doorway, with its lettering above, the band which emphasizes a kind of architrave embracing the span of the main front, and the bases and caps of its pillars. Powerful floodlights illuminate the whole after dark.[7]

The facade was 200ft long and the coloured tiling and faience were by Carter & Co. According to *The Builder*, 'This factory is remarkable not only for its architectural treatment but for the rapidity with which the work was designed and erected. The architects were allowed only three weeks in which to prepare the contract drawings and the time from the beginning of the work on site by the contractors to the making of the first tyre was only eighteen weeks.'[8] *The Architects' Journal* records a construction time of seven months from the laying of the foundations to the production of the first tyre, but whatever the length of time, as the *Journal* continues; 'Such an achievement bespeaks the closest co-operation between architect, contractors and factory engineers, assisted by the employment of building materials rendered available by modern scientific research.' This last comment was in reference to the steel-framing and reinforced concrete constructions. 'The undertaking represents, in fact, something of a triumph in concrete construction, equally from the aesthetic and the utilitarian points of view.'[9] In this instance Carter & Co.'s technical contribution was in the traditional building material. Stylistically the design of the Paris exhibition of 1925 was making itself felt in architecture as in pottery, and on the Firestone factory these embellishments give the building an exotic touch of richness, in contrast with the strictly industrial works behind.

Three years later, in 1932, the Hoover factory was completed at Perivale. This building was also designed by Wallis, Gilbert & Partners and, as before, Carter & Co. were the contractors and fixers for the decorative faience and, in this case, the terrazzo flooring.[10] As with the Firestone factory, the utilitarian works were masked by an administrative block fronted by a stylish facade of columns, here interspaced with windows. The main entrance was the most striking feature, being emphasized with a fan-shaped panel in polychrome faience and gold. A more mundane contri-

The tea-room at the East Quay works, showing Harold Stabler teaware, Studland shape, wall tiles adapted from designs by Edward Bawden and a faience wall panel probably designed by John Adams. *c.* 1933. *Poole Pottery Ltd.*

bution to this building by Carter's was in the tiling of the cloak-
rooms, toilets, kitchens, canteen, etc. Two other factories in this
area which Carter's worked on were the Pyrene and Gillette
buildings.[11]

As a third example of Carter & Co.'s work at this time, the De
La Warr Pavilion, completed at Bexhill in Sussex, in 1935, provides
a complete contrast of purpose. Interestingly, where Carter & Co.
supplied elaborately decorative faience for the industrial buildings,
Erich Mendelsohn and Serge Chermayeff, the two eminent architects for this intended leisure centre, required nothing more from
the Tileworks than brown floor tiling, cream wall tiles and straw-
coloured terrazzo. The external walls were rendered in a special
'non-crazing cement'[12] and where Carter's Ceramic Marble was
tested and proven as a successful material in withstanding seaside
conditions, the special cement, Cullamix, did not have the same
qualities.[13] The stylistic difference between this building and the
two factories represents the conflict between the Jazz Modern
school which caught on to the French fashion as a sort of instantly
contemporary style, and the purist International Modern movement, whose sources were drawn from the more lasting and intel-
lectual developments in Germany and Scandinavia.

In yet another field, Carter's had been doing some repair work
in the late 1920s, on the earlier Underground stations in London.
These were designed by Leslie W. Green around the turn of the
century and used dark red- and green-glazed faience by firms such
as G. Woolliscroft & Son of Hanley. By the 1930s Carter's were
beginning to fulfil all the tiling faience work, both on newly built
or re-vamped stations themselves. Cyril Carter and Harold Stabler's contacts in the Design and Industries Association were
undoubtedly bearing fruit, for Frank Pick, the vice-chairman of
London Passenger Transport Board, was the president of the
D.I.A. in 1933, having been a member since 1915. Charles Holden,
the innovatory architect of the new tube stations, had also been a
member since the foundation year, and certainly he and Cyril were
more than acquaintances and fellow members, for the architect
presented Cyril with a chair of his own design to mark the
friendship.[14]

Carter & Co. were also employed in modernizing the older
stations, and the decorative features for these were designed by
Reginald Till and Harold Stabler. Stabler designed a series of

moulded relief tiles with various symbols and images including Westminster, St Paul's Cathedral and the Crystal Palace, all signed on the front with a moulded letter 'S' and spray-glazed in creams and off-whites. These were used mainly on the City Line improvements and may still be seen there.

Following the *Queen Mary* contract, Carter's were commissioned to work on the sister liner, the *Queen Elizabeth*, which was completed at the outbreak of the Second World War. The Pottery provided decorative wares for both ships, honey-coloured pots for the *Queen Mary* and for the *Queen Elizabeth* probably a series of tall vases in classical style, which they covered with their mottled Shagreen glaze.[15] One of these is in the Pottery's own collection. The Tileworks were again responsible for the swimming pool areas, and in particular the Turkish baths where Reginald Till's tubeline designs were employed. Carter's previous experience with the technical complications of making and fixing faience and tiling to the special curves of a ship meant that they had acquired a certain pre-eminence in the field by this time.

One further area in which Carter & Co. figured largely was in hospital tiling. Their massive production of quality cream- and white-glazed tiles meant that they were among architects' first choice of contractors for hygienic surfacing of operating theatres, kitchens and laboratories. Once contracted for this type of standard work they were also commissioned to produce decorative panels for other areas in the hospitals, particularly for children's wards. The list of hospitals where they fulfilled this type of contract is long, and the schemes varied. In the children's ward of the Royal Free Hospital, for instance, Dora Batty's Nursery Rhyme designs and Joseph Roelants' Dutch tiles were used around the fireplace in standard style. In 1935 Carter & Co. produced an advertising booklet on their 'Picture Tiles for Hospitals' which featured their work in children's wards during the first five years of the decade and which showed a great advance in awareness both of the possibilities and the need for planned and cohesively designed tile schemes.

The west wing of the Middlesex Hospital was rebuilt in 1930, and while Carter's made many thousands of yards of plain tiling for the main building, for which the architect was Alner W. Hall,[16] the decoration of the babies' ward was to be of special interest and was the subject of a national competition. The winning designs

were by Haydn Jensen and were based on fairground scenes set in that romantic unspecified period somewhere between the medieval and the eighteenth century, where costume and architectural styles are untroubled by fact or historical accuracy. The designs were broadly conceived in a poster-like manner and caused Carter's to work in a style which was largely unfamiliar to them.

In 1935 a decorative scheme for twelve panels for the Princess Elizabeth Ward of the King Edward Hospital at Ealing were completed. These are particularly featured in the booklet as the latest and the most prestigious contract, and they are also mentioned in *The Builder*. Since neither publication credits the designer it seems likely that he or she was on the staff of the Tileworks. The main subjects this time were taken from nursery rhymes, but are quite unlike the Dora Batty versions. Two further panels were made which were specially authorized by the Duke and Duchess of York (later King George VI and Queen Elizabeth). The first depicted a small thatched house presented to Princess Elizabeth (now Queen Elizabeth II) by the Welsh nation, and the second showed Princess Elizabeth and Princess Margaret Rose standing by the sundial outside the house. Another scheme, for a Noah's Ark and a delightful series of comical characters, also unattributed, was destined for the Kent and Sussex Hospital at Tunbridge Wells.. For some reason they were not used there, but instead became part of the King Edward Hospital decorations. This hospital is particularly rich in painted tiles and there is a second decorated ward, named after Prince Edward of Kent, which contains a further series of ten scenes based on nursery rhymes. While the designer and painter for these appear to be the same as for the Princess Elizabeth Ward, the Noah's Ark mural is in a more sketchy, less formal style. Carter's completed the walls with plain tiles and inserted a panel in raised outline lettering, over each bed or cot, indicating the individual benefactors.[17]

In the early 1930s two of London's most famous hotels were renovated, Claridge's and the Savoy. The pressure for this came from Dame Bridget D'Oyley Carte, daughter of the then owner. The designers were Oswald Milne and Basil Ionides, and Carter's

Mosaic panel designed by Clifford and Rosemary Ellis for the British Art in Industry Exhibition, Royal Academy, in 1935. *Architectural Review, 1935.*

fulfilled the commission for the bathrooms in both hotels. The tiling ranged from plain restrained colours to mosaic patterning in a crackled turquoise and gold (this last in the Savoy). In addition C.S.A. provided some of the decorative ware for the Savoy. The pieces were of various types, including vases decorated with green-sprayed Picotee bands.[18]

Like the Pottery, the Tileworks continued to exhibit at trade fairs throughout the period and made it their policy to show the best of their forthcoming and current production on stands which were not merely a support for the display but which had some design merit in their own right. In 1933 their stand at the Building Trades Exhibition was featured in the *Architectural Review* in a small article pressing for collaboration between architects and exhibiting industrial firms. Carter & Co., having used the architects Stanley Hall and Easton and Robertson, were selected for special mention and illustration. Robertson had completed designs for the Pottery tea-rooms only shortly before. The writer finished with a plea: 'It is well worth spending seventy to a hundred pounds in prizes to secure some good architectural brains for the solution of a problem of advertising display. To the comment "Prove it!", the illustrations in these pages are the best possible reply.'[19] Parallel with C.S.A., Carter & Co. Ltd were consciously maintaining a progressive image. It is probable that this was Cyril's responsibility and in the same year he commissioned Robertson for a third project, possibly as an extension of the tea-room contract. The main staircase from the tile and pottery showrooms on the East Quay was rebuilt, with the showrooms, and again Carter & Co. were featured in an article devoted to the best and most enlightened patronage and design.[20] Robertson designed a stairway of impressive proportions which was faced with Carter's tiles in broken fawn (in a new 12" × 8" size) and jade green with dark green and black terrazzo, and ceramic mosaic flooring.

This company awareness of the importance of good design meant that the Tileworks, like the Pottery, also exhibited at the various decorative art and design exhibitions. They too contributed to British Art in Industry at the Royal Academy in 1935. Their most impressive entry was in the form of a large panel from a design by John Farleigh. The figures are over-life size and the relief modelling was by Harry Brown. The jointing was done in the style of stained glass, cutting round the edges of the figures where possible, and

Tiles by

CARTER

To the careless eye, many tiles must look alike. But cheerful, ever-clean colour finds instant response, and perhaps nowhere so much as in a floor. This **CARTER** teashop floor was done in four simple, refreshing colours; two sizes of tiles were used to give ·textural interest.'' Definitely a first-class floor. Remember that the famous **CARTER** floor tiles are supplied in a number of interesting colour shades, and that there are a variety of sizes to choose from. Write for information to **CARTER & CO. LTD.**, Poole, Dorset, or to 29 Albert Embankment, S.E.11, giving particulars of your problem.

Advertisement for Carter & Co. showing plain floor tiles and also Studland shape coffee ware, designed by Harold Stabler. 1938. *Architectural Review, 1938.*

was sensitively achieved by Reginald Till who regarded this technique as his speciality and this particular panel as one of his finest.

Naturally the Tileworks also benefited from Cyril's Design Association contacts and Stabler's connections in the exhibition field. The last pre-war exhibition with which the Tileworks were involved was one arranged by the Council for Art and Industry under Frank Pick. This was another in the series begun with silver and pottery, in which historical examples were shown alongside contemporary production. The exhibition was held at the Victoria and Albert Museum in 1939 and Cyril was on the committee which was chaired by Stabler. With this representation the Tileworks could hardly fail to make a good showing, and in fact they had an almost embarrassingly large proportion of exhibition space, particularly in the section devoted to hand-painted tiles. Other tile-makers represented by production included Pilkington, T. & R. Boote, Minton Hollins, Doulton & Co., H. & R. Johnson, H. & G. Thynne, Richards, Packard & Ord. Individual studio tile-makers such as Stella Crofts, T. S. Haile, Dora Billington and the Leach Pottery were also given space. Carter's themselves showed Stabler's London Transport tiles, some aerographed chevron patterns of the type used in the tea-rooms, and a selection of coloured tubelined and incised tiles designed by Truda and by Reginald Till, and close in style to those used on the Cunard liners. In the hand-painted section were various examples such as Fish by Arthur Nickols, and flowers based on Truda's ever-popular motifs, with close alternatives by Reginald Till. Also included were panels of Stabler's own Waterbirds and Dora Batty's Nursery Rhymes and Nursery Toys of fifteen years earlier. In addition, matching and contrasting plain tiles were sent in to the Museum with two faience letters (unspecified), the third one having spoilt in the kiln.[21] A special range, Florida, was submitted, developed by Reginald Till. The thick buff body was decorated with a random quantity of green, blue or salmon which was 'thrown' on and, when fired, had a mottled sunburst effect.[22] From the late 1920s Carter's had been making vitreous tiles with a speckled effect formed with grains of a different coloured clay, and the Florida range appears to have been a more unpredictable version. This effect is now a standard production. The tile panel based on Edward Bawden's Poole town design was also proposed for exhibition, but was rejected eventually as having the 'air of an adver-

The offices of Carter & Co. (London) Ltd, 29, Albert Embankment, showing, above, the dolphin and kiln symbol designed by Arthur Nickols. *c.* 1930, when the building was altered and modernised. *Pilkington Tiles Ltd.*

tisement'.[23] The historic tiles shown were drawn from the Museum's own collections, and illustrated styles and techniques from the medieval times to the nineteenth century.

By the end of the decade the Tileworks were producing a vast range of wall and floor tiles, both technically and artistically. They had experimented successfully with methods from hand-painting to stencilling, spraying, tubelining, incising and moulding. The works had been improved and added to; the floor tile factory (the

Architectural Pottery) had been largely re-built with a Williamson tunnel kiln installed in 1927. The wall tile factory (the White Works) had put in a third Dressler kiln in 1937. A second Dressler had been constructed in 1927, since the original kiln continued to suffer a multitude of problems mainly due to high tides saturating the foundations and wiring, and cutting off the underground flue. Some efforts were made to overcome these difficulties and the flue was re-routed overhead. However, it simply developed new eccentricities, and other problems included frequent snarling-up of the rollers under the trucks which meant that the men, primitively protected with wet sacks and tea-leaves, had to crawl into the hot kiln to free the jam. If the blockage was too far in, the kiln had to be left to cool right down and yet more production time was lost.[24]

The Group expanded and in 1928 Carter & Co. Ltd became a public company. It was joined by Carter & Co. (London) Ltd, and Carter, Stabler & Adams Ltd (in which they already had a controlling interest), and Art Pavements and Decorations Ltd. In 1931 J. H. Barrett and Co. (1927) Ltd joined the Group and one year later, in 1932, the Marbolith Flooring Co. Ltd was purchased.[25] These additions meant that Carter & Co. were able to undertake every type of ceramic or ceramic-allied surfacing and flooring, even extending, with Marbolith, to composition and cork flooring. This production, with Carter & Co. (London) Ltd, made possible a complete service from drawing out the design to ordering the materials and 'fixing' the tiling to faience. Their London drawing office was serviced by a team of representatives who, during the 1920s, had acquired their own contracts and ordered the work individually. Around 1931 this method was more sensibly resolved and a contracts department was set up on Ronald Cole's suggestion.[26] Orders were brought in as a block – the next twenty public houses or dozen shops – and draughtsmen went to the site to see the building or the builder. Drawings were then made and orders sent down to the Tileworks for the materials. In this way they fulfilled contracts for public houses owned by Charrington's, Mann, Crossman and Paulin's, Hoare and Co., Courage's and Benskin's, all of whom had standard designs. Watney Coombe and Reid & Co. were exceptional in that they experimented continually with different schemes.[27] With this network of operations, Carter & Co. were one of the largest firms in their field at the outbreak of war.

8
1945-1964

The Pottery: new lines
and post-war developments

I N 1943 Harry Trethowan reviewed the pottery industry's contribution to war-time essential domestic production. He wrote that:

Here is a chance for the Potter to design and make 'something good'
rather than 'something different', for him to direct and stimulate public
taste rather than adopt the doubtful attitude of trying to suit all tastes.

  The palette is clean, decoration and colour have been banned, and the
designer is free from the clamour of the distributor, he is free to work his
will, and to do what he has long desired to do – present to the public
examples of work to which the Potteries have never before had sufficient
time to give full attention.[1]

His article was illustrated with Utility wares produced by Wedgwood, Moorcroft, Beswick, Copeland-Spode and Carter, Stabler
& Adams.

  During the war the C.S.A. workforce dwindled to a skeleton
team headed by Ernest Baggaley. John Adams was frequently
absent as his health began to fail. The Poole showrooms were used
as immigration offices, leased to Imperial Airways[2] and the health
inspectorate. Situated on the quay, they and the Tileworks were
ideally positioned and Cyril Carter joined the counter-espionage
work and interviewed would-be immigrants.[3] Despite these difficulties C.S.A. gained a high reputation for their domestic production at this time. The Utility ware was designed and modelled by
Baggaley. He used the existing Streamline saucer but rethought
and remodelled the remaining complete domestic range. He
ordered 20 tons of frit, made a special glaze, and for several years
produced quantities of the plain cream-white ware for which there

Sherbourne dinner ware, designed by John Adams and available in a choice of two colours with white. 1950. *Poole Pottery Ltd.*

was a great demand. The final firing in each batch was taken to the showrooms still hot, and sold immediately. Plates sold for 7d., a cup and saucer for 1s. 1d. – not the cheapest available but generally agreed to be the best quality.[4] The sale showrooms were opened for just one day a week and queues a hundred yards long waited for the doors to open.

In 1945 Ernest Baggaley left to establish his own pottery works. He began with a small gas kiln in which he fired cast electrical elements, and later he extended the works to include four large kilns. He too made earthenware, then a type of vitrified, translucent ware using felspar; he subsequently developed this as a stoneware, and now produces a fine porcelain, always his ultimate goal, at the Branksome China Works, Fordingbridge, in the New Forest.[5]

The years immediately after the war were a time of staff changes at C.S.A. Many did not return to their vacated jobs, while others took the opportunity to leave. Gertie Gilham was one who left (in 1950) and she, with others, went to work for Baggaley at Branksome.[6]

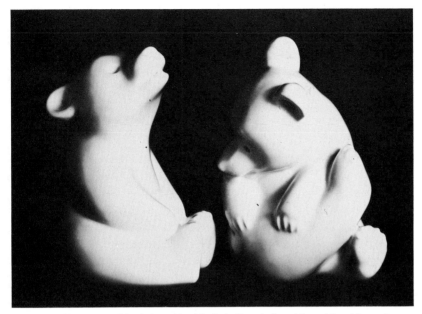

Pair of bears, possibly designed by Marjorie Drawbell and issued in white and
brown glazes. *c.* 1950–55. *Victoria & Albert Museum.*

A new works manager, Roy T. Holland, was appointed in 1945.
Holland came from Stoke-on-Trent and had ten pre-war years'
experience in the Potteries. He went to C.S.A. straight from the
R.A.F. and, on his appointment, was told that his first task was to
redevelop the East Quay works. The Pottery was largely derelict
at this point. A small part had been working under Baggaley and
some effort had been made to restart the production of decorated
ware. However, the larger area was deserted. The solid old kilns,
which had been used to fire the Carter & Co. structural ceramic,
had served as air-raid shelters and at the end of the war the little
work of this type still made was finally transferred to Hamworthy.
David Carter, Cyril's son, who was an architect, joined the firm
in 1945 and he, with Holland, worked on sketch plans for the East
Quay rebuilding. Post-war building regulations prevented them
from demolishing the whole site and so development was piecemeal, as it had always been, incorporating with the old building
the new Gibbons twin-tunnel electric kiln for glaze and biscuit
firing. Advice was taken from Stoke-on-Trent architects and work
started in 1946. The structural ceramic kilns were demolished and

Jesse Carter's eccentric building with its floor-tile roof and pit prop supports was demolished. According to a contemporary witness, the outer, quayside wall was retained.[7]

While this was taking place plans were made towards stepping up production and improving the marketing side. Restrictions on the home sale of decorated ware were not lifted until 1952 and so foreign markets were essential business. C.S.A.'s export contacts were not extensive. A few were revived after the war but it was imperative that they were built up to a wider and richer network and that at the same time the production of coloured tableware and ornamental pieces should be re-established. It was decided to reintroduce some of the two-tone colour range; four were produced – Sepia and Mushroom (C54), Seagull and Ice Green (C57), Sky Blue and Magnolia (C84), and Peach Bloom and Seagull (C97). Under the post-war regulations these glazes had to be developed to incorporate a lower lead content than previously, and in this form they reappeared under a new range name, Twintone. In addition, John Adams designed the slip-faced ware Cameo, and also a dinner and tea ware shape, Sherborne. This was chiefly distinguished by the cut-away angle to the cup foot, and was available by 1950 for export only. Altogether there were 61 shapes in Shell Pink or Celadon Green with Ivory White.[8] Truda Carter's hand-painted wares were also continued, but under the new range name Traditional Poole. A few new patterns were introduced, probably by Truda. One, Spring, was based on an earlier design of a leaping stag; Strasbourg, again, was an updated interpretation of her pre-war flower designs. Leaf was an entirely new design.[9]

These decorated wares were made solely for the export market at this time. Board of Trade rulings allowed seconds to be sold at home, however, and this was done primarily through the Pottery's own shop. Sound ware which had been stored since 1942 was not recognized under this licence, and consequently was not available to home retailers who were allowed to sell Utility ware only. It was not an easy task producing these lines immediately after the war, with a partly skilled, partly trained workforce, and a mixture of pre-war, makeshift and new equipment. The new Gibbons kiln was not operable until 1949.

While the workforce itself had changed considerably, the senior staff were also undergoing certain revolutions. Harold Stabler died in 1945 and Phoebe had not worked there for some years. Truda

Two carafes, the shapes of which were designed by Claude Smale.
Left: decoration designed by A. B. Read;
right: decoration designed by Lucien Myers. *c.* 1953. *Victoria & Albert Museum.*

Carter reached retirement age in March 1950 and proposed to continue to work for the company, but at home. She continued in this capacity under the title of design consultant, but made few significant contributions to the design stocks after the war. John Adams went through a very difficult time. He was not strong and knew that the time was approaching when he would have to be replaced. He felt a deep concern for the Pottery which had been his life for thirty years, and for the people with whom he worked. Discussions took place between him and Cyril on the directions future design should take and on the best method of finding and appointing a satisfactory person. During the final two or three years of the 1940s C.S.A. was not so much steered as pushed and worried through emotional, personality and commercial problems. Finally, in 1950, the management was settled and all vacancies, except for the still untenanted design post, were filled. John Adams retired from his managing directorship at the end of 1949 and from the post of art director in May 1950. As managing director he was

Group of coronation ware designed by A. B. Read. 1953. *Poole Pottery Ltd.*

easily replaced by Lucien Myers, who had joined the firm in the same year.[10] His previous experience as editor of the *Pottery and Glass* trade journal, and in the wholesale and retail trades, made him especially useful in establishing new market contacts. However, Adams' disappearance from the design field left a gap which took many years to fill satisfactorily. He and Truda had carried the Pottery, to a great extent, since its establishment in 1921, and their departure left C.S.A. without a strong or individual team.

In the meantime, business was at least progressing with the lines in production. Utility ware was made for the last time in May 1950 and the Sherborne and Streamline shapes were both successful. In fact, at that point sales were exceeding production. Overseas markets were still struggling: Canada, Norway, Sweden, Italy,

View of a display showing a range of 'free form' and other vases designed by
A. B. Read. 1958. *Poole Pottery Ltd.*

South Africa, Rhodesia and some of the West Indies all bought
Poole pottery, but Europe and the U.S.A. had not proved at all
receptive. However, for a while it seemed that there were enough
shapes and decorations to sustain the works for some time,
although discussions on the possibility of a design unit were already
under way.

In 1951 the Festival of Britain was held on the South Bank in
London, and this provided the first and only major opportunity
for the Pottery to demonstrate its recovery and promise for the
future. C.S.A. showed a special display of wares and mounted a
demonstration of the in-glaze painting technique which they continued to employ on their Traditional Poole and other hand-
painted ranges. Four of the paintresses spent a fortnight in London

as demonstrators, and a van was driven up regularly from Poole to keep them supplied with ware and colours.[11]

In 1950 an appointment had been made to the design post. Claude Smale, a student taken directly from the Royal College of Art, joined the staff in July with Ruth Pavely as assistant and Truda still nominally as design consultant. The period of his appointment was brief – about six months – and his main contribution was with designs in connection with the Festival of Britain. A licence was applied for in December 1950 for the production and sale of Festival souvenirs to the value of £5,000. Post-war restrictions were still in force and while it was possible to sell a certain amount of ornamental ware in Magnolia White, teapots, coffee-pots and milk jugs in plain-coloured glazes (the Streamline range with two-colour glazes, for instance), and the Sherborne range in plain-coloured slip, all production was under licence only. Special ranges such as souvenirs involved further application to the Board of Trade. By March the licence still had not been issued and export orders were so great that there was no longer any production space for souvenir ware. Finally only a limited quantity was produced under the normal home trade 'fancies' licence.[12] Under these circumstances C.S.A. made a number of presentation pieces, many using pre-war shapes by John Adams. The decoration was designed by Claude Smale based on the arms of the relevant town or county with flower motifs symbolizing the British Isles.[13] The Pottery exhibited some of their standard production in various sections of the Festival display. In the 'Homes and Gardens, Entertainment at Home' area Sherborne teaware was included. Unspecified tea and dinner ware was also shown in the 'Kitchen Storage' section.[14]

This first appointment was not a success, and following Smale's departure a new designer was found – Alfred Burgess Read, appointed to serve both the Tileworks and the Pottery and to head the proposed design unit. A. B. Read was a Royal Designer for Industry and had had a distinguished career working for Troughton & Young, the lighting firm, well known for its advanced designs in the 1930s. He had studied metalwork at the Royal College of Art between 1919 and 1923 and consequently must have been the last of Harold Stabler's many ex-R.C.A. contacts. Soon after his marriage in 1923 and a student scholarship to Italy, he had designed some kitchen tile subjects for Carter & Co.[15] This was quickly followed by the setting-up of the Clement Dane Advertising Studio in the Strand, London, with some friends. He then spent about two years working for the French lighting firm Baguès and finally, after this whirlwind career, he was offered a Directorship by Troughton & Young in 1925, when he was only twenty-seven. He stayed with them until the Second World War. During the 1920s and 1930s the Reads' continuing contact with Poole was with Cyril Carter, through the Design and Industries Association and the Arts Club. They frequently went to stay at 'Yaffle Hill', for which Troughton & Young had carried out the lighting contract. In late 1951 this established friendship resulted in his being offered the vacant design post.[16]

In 1952 the special or studio wares were in production and a new printed backstamp was introduced to replace the impressed mark of 'Carter, Stabler & Adams Ltd', which had been in use since 1925. The new stamp incorporated the dolphin insignia, which had been employed only once before, for a brief period around 1900–8. The use of the impressed mark was abandoned and instead the new mark was simply lettered 'Poole, England'. The special and decorative wares were additionally marked 'Hand

Streamline tableware, with updated handle to the cup and knob on the jug lid, glazed in Twintone colours. *c.* 1956. *Poole Pottery Ltd.*

Plate designed by Ann Read and painted by Ruth Pavely in green, blue, browns and red, showing Cyril Carter's house, 'Yaffle Hill'. This was one of a set of four presented to him on completing fifty years with the company. 1955. *Private collection.*

Made, Hand Decorated'.[17] While the Pottery had always been known as C.S.A. within the trade and between the two works, the public had referred to it as 'Poole' and its production as 'Poole pottery' since 1921 and even before. The name of the Pottery was not officially altered to Poole Pottery until 1962.

Early in 1951 various experiments were carried out on new or earlier techniques and glazes, including sgraffito decoration, towards the introduction of the special ranges. Some of these were put into production and were included when C.S.A. began a series of exhibitions at the Ceylon Tea Centre in London's Regent Street. The first of these shows was held in 1953 and was opened by the architect Sir Hugh Casson. Twintone tableware was laid in place settings together with glass made by James Powell & Sons, White-friars Glassworks.[18] Ornamental ware in Chinese Blue, Chinese Green, various eggshell glazes and Magnolia White was shown in company with A. B. Read's designs for hand-painted vases, carafes and coronation wall plaques. Read produced a number of designs for coronation ware, mostly based on the royal coat-of-arms, the

Ann Read decorating dishes to her own designs. 1952–6. *Poole Pottery Ltd.*

E II R monogram and various celebratory phrases, surrounded with either calligraphic patterning or coloured stripes.

About a year after his appointment A. B. Read was joined at Carter's by his daughter, Ann. She had studied fine art at Chelsea School of Art and had since done a variety of drawing, painting and teaching jobs. Ill-health in her youth limited her chances of belatedly starting and sustaining a career in fiercely competitive and physically demanding professions, and so her talents were given scope at Poole. She joined the Tileworks first, working briefly on tile painting under Phyllis Butler. She then moved to the Pottery where she was taught the art of painting on the powdery, pink, unfired glaze by Ruth Pavely. She found that her previous training gave her no advantage in this technique and, like every other trainee paintress, she had to acquire the specialized skill through practice. In addition to working as a paintress she also made some original designs. Very few of these became standard commercial production and instead most were issued over some years in special or limited ranges; several were still available in 1958.[19] Heal's were still buying from Poole at this period and their buyer, Mr Lowe, ordered from her thirty plates decorated with various scenes and landscapes. Others were made specially, in even smaller batches. In 1955 Cyril Carter had completed fifty years with the company and Ann Read and Ruth Pavely planned to make a personal gift to him. They made a secret expedition to 'Yaffle Hill' to draw Cyril's house. A plate, decorated with a view of 'Yaffle Hill', was smuggled into the glost kiln and was seen, quite by chance, by Lucien Myers. He was so impressed that the one plate was augmented to four, decorated with suitable motifs, and these were presented to Cyril at a party held in his honour. A further special order from Heal's did become standard production. In her last year at Poole, 1956, Ann was asked to make a design using the currently fashionable bamboo motif. She applied it in white on to a black ground on the newly modified Streamline shape tableware.[20]

While Ann Read was working on plate designs and as a paintress, her father was adding to the ornamental range with a series of handsomely patterned vases. Like his daughter, he had had no training in the pottery industry and many of his designs were found to be unsuitable without some adaptation. In this way they lost much of their original style but nevertheless they stand as a distinctive and important group. Some of these patterns were also used on Streamline tableware, fancies (egg cups, nut bowls, condiment sets, jam pots) and giftware (*hors d'oeuvre* sets, butter pats and biscuit barrels, curiously known by the American description, 'cookie jars'). The A. B. Read patterns included Featherdrift, Ariadne, Constellation and Ripple, and were painted on the wares listed above which were also decorated with the Trudiana patterns based on Truda Carter's flower motifs. All these patterns were painted on matt white glazes and teamed with contrasting Sepia, Terracotta Red and Glacier Blue glazes, among other colours. In 1955 Read went into hospital suffering from tuberculosis. Until that date he had been largely concerned with pattern design, but while he was in hospital and in a sanatorium he produced shape designs, particularly for flower vases. This was due as much to his wife's interest and expertise in flower arranging as to demand from the Pottery catering for a public equally interested in this fashionable and popular pastime.[21] These new designs included those known as 'free form' which were distinguishable by their elliptical,

Group of three plates designed by Ann Read. 1952–6. *Photograph: Private collection.*

The updated Streamline tableware shape with decoration designed by
Ann Read. 1956. *Photograph: Private collection.*

asymmetrical shapes. They were either decorated with hand-
painted patterns applied by Ruth Pavely or plain glazed in Black
Panther, white or other colours.

A year later Ann Read also contracted tuberculosis and with the
departure of both Reads from the Pottery side, Poole was once
again left without a resident designer. On his release from the
sanatorium, A. B. Read continued at the Tileworks for a brief time
during 1957–8 and then returned to Troughton & Young. At Poole,
the design unit had developed into no more than an extension of
responsibility and opportunity for talented and experienced staff
such as Ruth Pavely. No other specialist designers had been
appointed. In 1958 Robert Jefferson arrived and this marked a
turning point in the Poole production. Jefferson had previously
worked with the short-lived decorative production made by
Buller's Ltd, near Hanley – a firm which normally specialized (and
still does) in industrial wares.[22] After a year spent there while he
was still a student at Stoke-on-Trent School of Art, he won a
scholarship to the Royal College of Art. This was followed with a
teaching post at a school at Gravesend and then eighteen months
at the Odney Pottery in Cookham, at that time owned by the John
Lewis Partnership. In 1956, when the Partnership appointed a
new chairman, the Pottery was shut down and Jefferson freelanced
for a period before taking up a teaching post at Burslem School of
Art. Finally, in 1958, he applied for the job at Poole and became
their first designer trained and experienced in the pottery industry
since John Adams' arrival.[23]

A. B. Read was still working for the Tileworks occasionally, but
Jefferson on the pottery side found himself entirely alone and
independent. His first task was to draw every shape in production
for the shapes book and advertising leaflets. This work and arranging the showroom and other displays occupied him completely for
his first year, apart from the design of a few accessories. In his
second year at the Pottery he revolutionized the tableware range
with an entirely new design, Contour. With its upswept handles
and vigorous body shape, it was Poole's first truly post-war tableware production. The Streamline shape, an established popular
seller, was still continued, but the adaptations to knobs and handles did not disguise the fact that it was a pre-war design. The
Contour range was an instant success, and was made in four Twintone glazes – Mushroom and Sepia (C54), Seagull and Ice Green

(C57), Dove Grey and Sky Blue (C104), Brazil and Sweet Corn (C107) and in the new Cameo glazes, converted from the original slip finishes, Blue Moon and Celeste.

Following this success Jefferson produced a printed pattern, Pebble, especially designed for the Murray Curvex machine recently acquired by the Pottery. The printing technique was based on what was known as the 'gelatine bomb'. The parabolic bomb-shaped gelatine was lowered and pressed on to an inked copper sheet etched with the design, and from there on to the waiting plate. This was the only pattern designed for the machine; its use was never developed and instead remained limited to Streamline coupe-shaped plates and similar surfaces.[24]

Streamline teaware, with updated knob and 'Trudiana' painted decoration based on Truda Carter's floral designs. *c.* 1956. *Poole Pottery Ltd.*

Late in 1960 Poole, like other potteries, caught on to the 'oven-to-table' ware trend which had come from America. Robert Jefferson designed their range – both the shapes and the decoration – and the pieces were issued complete with a heater stand for one of the casseroles. Two printed patterns were produced, the first being Lucullus in which the motifs were blackberry and apple, a cockerel, sweetcorn, eggs, prawns and scallops, peapods and leaves, peapods and cauliflowers, marrows and mushrooms. The second pattern was called Herb Garden and its motifs were sage, bay, basil, thyme, parsley, clove, borage, caraway and mint. The patterns were matched with the plain glaze Blue Moon, and later with the lighter blue Celeste. A further colour was also launched with the new production – Heather Rose, a deep pink. This was not successful and so was discontinued. The ovenware was introduced at a special exhibition held at the Tea Centre and a trade journal reported on its success eighteen months later:

Both ranges have the unmistakable Poole quality about them. They exhibit the same deliberate confidence that it is the mark of the professional industrial designer which can always be seen throughout the entire

Contour tableware, designed by Robert Jefferson. 1959. *Photograph: Private collection.*

Poole range of productions from their establishment 42 years ago. The ovenware shapes, though they have been greatly admired, have been subject to criticism on the score that the plain colours are somewhat austere in this day and age. This view, which is not necessarily shared by all Poole admirers, can no longer be sustained, and the two new patterns will assuredly have a bright future both at home and in the overseas market.

Carter, Stabler & Adams report that, during the interval that has elapsed since the oven-to-table range was introduced, the number of items returned under the guarantee against breakage from oven heat has been less than half of one per cent. This would appear to be a remarkably good record, and amply confirms the manufacturer's claim regarding the high resistance of the ware to thermal shock. It should not be overlooked also that the shapes have the additional advantages of being both graceful and comparatively light in weight.[25]

Jefferson also designed special packaging to accompany the ware but this, like the Heather Rose colour, was abandoned due to some resistance from the retailers, worried about storage space, and the additional expense both of manufacture and to the customer. A new gas-fired Gibbons kiln, 119 ft long, was built specially to fire the ovenware and the expanded production generally, and was the

Oven-to-table ware decorated with the Lucullus pattern, designed in 1960 by Robert Jefferson, who also designed the herb jars in 1963. *Poole Pottery Ltd.*

third new kiln to be installed since the initial post-war development.[26] An article of some length appeared in the same trade
journal on the alterations necessary to the factory and equipment.
It ended with some explanation of the type of body used for the
new range:

It may not be generally known that the fine earthenware body that has
been used at Poole for the last ten years, both for general tablewares and
gift wares, already possesses a high resistance to thermal shock. Very
little modification to this body was consequently necessary in order to
transform it into a completely oven-proof body. Apart from this, only a
slight increase of firing temperature was found to be needed. Another
interesting factor is that the standard Poole tableware body has always
been fired well above normal earthenware temperature, being in fact,
about mid-way between earthenware and stoneware temperature. This
situation, together with the high content of flint and stone and other
materials, in addition to the Cornish, Devon and Dorset clays, produces
a semi-vitrified body of exceptional toughness.[27]

Jefferson's second tableware shape, Compact, made its appearance in about 1962 – its launching was delayed a year because of
limited production capacity. As the name suggests, it was neat and
space-saving. Storage considerations played a great part in its
design, a lesson learnt from the more extravagant lines of the

Compact tableware, designed by Robert Jefferson. *c.* 1962. *Photograph: Private
collection.*

Wall plaques with moulded, raised, line decoration, designed by Robert Jefferson.
1964. *Photograph: Private collection.*

Contour range. Most of the Compact shapes packed into their fellows. It was issued in white with Charcoal glaze and also Chestnut, which was a slip finish with a clear Crystal glaze over. These were added to in the following year with Choisya, an olive-green glaze. In the original design the lids were flat, without knobs, but after Jefferson left adaptations were made to this design, as they were to the Contour shape.

Jefferson's final contribution to the Pottery was to add to the tableware accessories, the giftware ranges and to the Studio range. In 1963 he was responsible for the design of spice jars with a matching tea, coffee and sugar canister. These were decorated with a type of in-glaze silk-screened patterning which he developed, in which the design was printed on to the tissue and the tissue then applied directly to the raw glaze and the print left to sink in for a minute or two. Of course, this method differs from the established technique of applying printed decoration to ceramic with tissue only in the use of silkscreen rather than an etched steel or copper plate, and with the in-glaze rather than the under or occasionally over-glaze application. It is more usual for the tissue to be allowed to burn off in the kiln, and this method was also used at the Tileworks. The new pattern was of an overall design of diamonds, known as Green Diamond, and the jars were sold with cork stoppers.

In 1963 Jefferson was joined by Tony Morris, newly qualified from Newport School of Art. Morris was first attached to Carter Tiles to work on the glazing of faience slabs to Jefferson's designs, and a group of these are now set into the Pottery wall. In Jefferson's last years at Poole, 1964 and 1965, he introduced new decorative wares in the Bokhara range of hand-painted and lined vases and covered jars with which he severed the painting department from the last clinging vestiges of the pre-war style. In 1964 a series of wall hangings appeared in the shape of angular, flat birds, fish and an exotic dagger. These were also produced as small trays with raised rims and were given coloured glazes which were floated over the moulded line decoration. The year 1965 saw the introduction of new Studio wares – elegant, elongated bottles with flattened rims, heavily textured bowls and stylishly decorated dishes and plates – a group of wares which he worked on with Tony Morris. These were subsequently produced as standard ware under the range name Delphis. Such hand-worked, moulded textures were

Helios lamp bases, designed by Robert Jefferson with Tony Morris. 1965.
Photograph: Private collection.

Studio wares, the dish and the vases on the left and far right designed by Robert
Jefferson, the centre vase designed by Tony Morris. 1965. *Photograph: Private
collection.*

Studio wares, the vase and bowl on the left probably designed by Tony Morris, and the vase on the right by Robert Jefferson. 1965. *Photograph: Private collection.*

also used on the Helios range of lamp bases, designed in the same year and supplied with smart, matching Perspex shades.

Jefferson left Poole in 1966. In eight years he had produced an astonishingly large quantity of highly successful wares of all types. At the end of that time promotion possibilities for any new ranges were saturated with existing lines selling well. He had provided the Pottery with the material to take it through to the 1970s and it was time for him to leave.[28]

In 1963 Cyril Carter resigned from the C.S.A. board, having reached the age of seventy-five; he finally retired in June 1965. Also during 1963, on 18 January, the Pottery's name was changed from Carter, Stabler & Adams Ltd to Poole Pottery. The following year the Tileworks merged with Pilkington Tiles Ltd. Although this had little effect on the Pottery at the time, it meant that eventually both the Tileworks and the Pottery were absorbed into the massive Thomas Tilling Group in 1971, when Pilkington's themselves were taken over. Since then the Pottery has continued as an autonomous unit within the Group.

9
1945-1964

The Tileworks: new lines and post-war developments

I N 1949 the firing of the terracotta and faience production was moved from Poole, where the kilns had been demolished, to Hamworthy. The manufacture of smaller pieces such as Stabler's galleons and garden figures, had long since finished and by the 1950s the work consisted mainly of war memorials and heraldic features for government and other offices in Britain and elsewhere. In the immediate post-war years much of the work involved patching and repairing war damage. An early job carried out by Reginald Till and Bill Eason was the repair work to the *Queen Mary* which, with its sister liner the *Queen Elizabeth*, had been requisitioned from Cunard for war work. It was government policy to repair any damage to property temporarily annexed during the war and while in this case Carter's were repairing their own original work, they were also frequently commissioned to carry out repair jobs which had been initially constructed by other firms. The *Queen Mary* was docked at Southampton for the repairs and Coombe, Till and Eason travelled there almost daily. Since it was impossible to cut out the large ceramic blocks, which were inset around steel fixtures, some of the damage was made good with paint.[1]

One of the most prestigious post-war jobs was the repair work done in 1948–9 to the bomb-damaged royal coat-of-arms on Buckingham Palace. Harry Brown, still chief modeller, worked on this with Bill Eason, reproducing the central shield surmounted by a crown, the four national emblems and a seated unicorn. The lion had survived intact. Harry Brown used 6 tons of clay to model this major sculptural piece; the crown alone weighted 15 cwt. and was fired as one complete section. The drying and firing were super-

intended by Billy Bryant, with whom Eason had worked on the
liners during the 1930s. The whole of the Buckingham Palace job
was in unglazed terracotta to fit in with the original stone.[2] Another
war damage repair job of interest was the production of replace-
ment encaustic tiles for St Stephen's Crypt in the Palace of
Westminster.[3]

As repair contracts became fewer the other type of faience work
became as much in demand after the Second World War as it had
after the First. Hamworthy provided a number of war memorials
and as part of the post-war building boom, coats-of-arms for new
schools and municipal buildings from Walthamstow and Islington
to New Zealand and Trinidad. In 1951 Carter & Co. Ltd produced, as one of their regular house publications, a booklet covering the Group's various areas of work including:

Purpose-made Work. Surfacing units which are unique to the designer's
scheme and purpose, and which for that reason must be individually
made, will always be of special significance. Such units include details
and embellishments such as cills and architraves as well as coats-of-arms
and other decorative devices.

Both the Poole tile factories have facilities for carrying out the finest
purpose-made work. In faience and terracotta they undertake to produce
virtually anything that can be produced in these media; whether in low
relief or free standing sculpture, and in any practicable colour and
texture.[4]

In addition to the advertised types of architectural decoration, by
1958 Carter's had taken over from Royal Doulton the work of
making various faience panels including those for the Greene King
brewery, originally modelled by George Kruger Gray, and the
London County Council encaustic enamelled plaques commem-
orating the houses of famous men and women.[5] The scheme was
begun by the Royal Society of Arts in 1875 and various types were
produced. By the time Carter's began the work the design was
established as a pale blue roundel inlaid with white lettering and
this highly skilled production has featured in a series of advertisements entered in the *Architects' Journal*, *The Builder* and the *R.I.B.A.
Journal* in 1960.

The 1951 Carter publication also mentioned the production of
mosaic. 'Another branch of purpose-made work concerns the making of tiles for use in specially designed mosaics. Probably there is
no work which brings crafts-man and artist designer into closer

Faience heraldic work for the repairs to war damage on Buckingham Palace, modelled by Harry Brown. *c.* 1950. *Pilkington Tiles Ltd.*

working contact, for, apart from the fine precision needed in fitting the tesserae, the workman must be able to envisage the design in its every detail of colour, texture and massing.'[6] By the end of the war Onslow had left and the mosaic department had stopped functioning. Cyril was particularly interested in mosaic and asked Leslie Coombe to restart the department. Before the war Coombe had worked in the drawing office and consequently had no practical experience of what had been an important part of Carter's work. Coombe began operating in much the same way as Onslow had before the war. He obtained a special permit to buy the treacle which, with gum arabic, had always been one of Onslow's glue ingredients for papering-up completed sections of mosaic pattern.

However, within a few years he had adopted more modern techniques and self-adhesive paper, easily peeled off, was used. Another acquisition, astonishingly not made until after the war, was of a special mosaic chopper. Previously the girls had used a hammer and chisel.[7] By the mid-1950s Carter & Co. were advertising a range of four different types of mosaic; production had obviously improved dramatically in a few years:

Ceramic mosaic is made from the same material as clay floor tiles and a colour range of about twenty colours is available. This mosaic is produced in 3/4" × 3/4" squares, 3/16" thick. There are about forty standard shades. The mosaic is cast in large sheets and broken down to the 3/4" × 3/4" size, producing the slight irregularity in each stone which is responsible for the characteristic effect.

Marble mosaic is supplied in 3/4" × 3/4" squares, 3/8" thick. This mosaic is cut from large slabs and it is not likely nor intended to be perfectly square. This is the type of mosaic used by the Romans in their tessellated paving and is equally suitable for square or 'fan pattern' designs. Colours are limited to the natural marble range and no vivid shades are available.

Venetian Glass mosaic is supplied in small irregular cubes hand-cut from sheet material. The cubes do not usually exceed 1/2" on face. This mosaic is not suitable for paving work except in special positions where there is no traffic and, generally speaking, is used only for decorative and pictorial work on walls. An extremely wide range of shades is produced.[8]

One area of work which has become increasingly important to the London company is that of conservation. Their years of experience, particularly with mosaic, have resulted in a flourishing sideline in the rescue of Roman mosaic pavements, in particular, and they have done a great deal of work in this field for St Albans, Bath and other originally Roman centres. Such conservation work is not confined to antique mosaic alone and the company also specialize in the removal of more recent tile panels from buildings about to be demolished, such as the decorative panels in the children's ward of St Thomas's Hospital, London.

While Carter & Co. welcomed 'opportunities for preparing special schemes for architects and designers'[9], they also offered the services of their design unit under the direction of A. B. Read. Although designers in other areas of tile work were employed by the firm in the early 1950s, Leslie Coombe seems to be the only

Mosaic work, repairs to war damage on the Plaza Cinema, Piccadilly, London. *c.* 1950. *Pilkington Tiles Ltd.*

person on Carter's staff who made designs for mosaic panelling or
floors until the establishment of the design unit. During the 1950s
outside designers were commisioned by architects. The artists
ranged from the African Kofi Antubam, who produced a distinctive
design for a community centre in Accra, Ghana, and worked with
the Carter team for some weeks at Hamworthy in 1951, to Edward
Bawden. Bawden was briefly tempted back into the Carter ceramic
field to design a coat-of-arms in black and white mosaic for the
High Commissioner's residence in Lagos, Nigeria, in 1961. The
effective contrast in this coat-of-arms lay not only in the two
opposing colours but also in the combined use of square and
hexagonal pieces as part of the design.[10] In England, Hans Tisdall
was persuaded by Cyril to produce a dramatic design for a panel
which was made for the Tileworks' own showroom in 1956. It was
entitled *Apotheosis* and was made face-up with the joints left
unfilled. This resulted in a dramatic surface texture which Tisdall
planned as part of the vigorous composition of a trumpeting angel
against a swirling elemental background.

While Coombe was re-establishing the mosaic department
another part of the works was developing a new branch. In about
1951 or 1952 Reginald Till left Carter's to join with John Bowman,
a former director, in a new pottery venture at Swanage. Before he
left, however, Till had done some experimental work in silk-screen
printing on tiles. A commission had been received from Ethiopia
in 1948 for decorated printed tiles, to be completed at very short
notice. Unfortunately the commission was not fulfilled in time but
the order prompted Till to search for ways of reproducing decoration on tiles in as speedy a way as possible. A major influence in
this early work was the designer Peggy Angus. At the time, she
was wholly engaged in teaching art at the North London Collegiate
School. A chance comment from a friend, the architect F. R. S.
Yorke, resulted in her search for a tile-manufacturing firm which
would be able to develop and use the lino- and potato-cut prints
she was producing so successfully through her school work. Yorke
was keen to use such designs, combining the colour and pattern
with architecture. After some investigation Peggy Angus arrived
at Carter's in 1949 or 1950. She had already done some work on

'Europa and the Bull', faience panel, designed by Joseph Ledger for the Carter &
Co. stand at the Building Trades Exhibition in 1953. *Pilkington Tiles Ltd.*

The royal coat-of-arms, mosaic mural designed by Edward Bawden for the Governor General's residence in Lagos, Nigeria. 1961. *Pilkington Tiles Ltd.*

lithographic transfers, adapting the process to take her lino-cut designs. The first experiments at Poole were taken direct from these cuts which were printed on to tissue. This was applied to the tile and fired.[11] After some experimentation a satisfactory silk-screening method was achieved. These early trials were developed and a provisional patent was put on the first successes. On Till's departure Jim Allen, who had been at the Tileworks since 1929, following his father into the firm, carried through many more technical improvements and Carter's became established as the first firm in Britain to use the method. Yorke used Peggy Angus's tiles based on the theme of waving banners, intended as symbolic of the post-war feeling, in the Susan Lawrence School at Poplar, in east London. In fact, Carter's connection with Yorke was well established and his architectural practice with Rosenberg and Mandall frequently employed Carter tiles. Peggy Angus was kept on by the Tileworks with a retaining fee until about 1960. Her

Screen-printed tile designs by Peggy Angus, from the Classic range. 1950–c.1955.
Illustration: Dolphin Ceramic Tiles Catalogue, 1964.

designs were featured on Carter's stand at the Building Trades Exhibition in 1951 which was also designed by Yorke. This was tiled with two types of her designs; one, an interchangeable series of waves, spots and lines (the range used in the Susan Lawrence School), and the other a simple, diagonally divided tile printed in various colours which could be assembled in various combinations. Throughout the 1950s designs based more closely on lino-cut techniques were also used, such as the cherries and birds series, the Welsh dragons combined with fleur-de-lis and leeks, and the stag with oak leaves and birds. They provided an attractive contrast with the more polished and clinical contemporary designs.

The Tileworks, like the Pottery, made some contribution to the Festival of Britain in 1951. They showed unspecified tiles in the bathroom part of the 'Homes and Gardens' section.[12] More importantly, however, was their contribution to the one permanent building put up on the South Bank, the Royal Festival Hall, designed by the architect to the London County Council, Robert Matthew and his deputy, J. L. Martin. The hall was decorated on the Hungerford Bridge side with pale blue and white tiles by Carter & Co. fixed by the London company. Carter & Co. were also involved in an experiment on this building using black, unglazed tiles which were put on the outside of the building in an attempt to conserve warmth within by absorbing outside heat. Unfortunately the experiment was too successful and the amount of heat absorbed affected the fixing material and resulted in loosening the tiles. The experiment was eventually abandoned. In addition to this work, Carter & Co. made up the decorative tiled panel mounted on the side of the Regatta Restaurant, which was designed by Victor Pasmore in the contemporary Abstract Expressionist manner, in the style of American artists such as Jackson Pollock. Across the river, Charing Cross underground station was refurbished as part of the celebrations and this work was undertaken by the London fixing company using plain tiles by Carter & Co.[13]

One interesting development during the Festival led to a design motif which was used on almost every material and now typifies

Carter & Co. stand, designed by F. R. S. Yorke for the Building Trades Exhibition in 1951, showing tiles designed by Peggy Angus including, spotlit on the highest wall, those used at the Susan Lawrence school by F. R. S. Yorke.
Photograph: Private collection.

Tile panel, designed by Ivor Kamlish and probably painted by Phyllis Butler, for a Fine Fare supermarket in Peckham. 1955–60. *Photograph: Private collection.*

the style of the period. A project was launched based on the current successful British research advances made in the study of crystallography and the consequent development of crystal structure diagrams. The scheme was intended to draw in various industries – textiles, ceramics, glass, etc. – to an involvement with this new, exciting field, by suggesting some of the diagrams as a starting point for pattern design. Thus Reginald Till designed a panel based on the diagram of the structure of zinc hydroxide.[14]

The London contracting company, responsible for a variety of services ranging from some designing to ordering and fixing materials both from Carter's and other tile makers, had its own particular problems after the war. Arthur Owen Carter, Alfred Carter's son, who had managed the London office for nearly fifty years, retired in 1947 and his place was taken by H. R. Hidden. During the next few years limitations on building were gradually lifted and rationing of materials meant that any contract had to be shaped to use the available tiling. Carter & Co. scored over many of their contemporaries by making 12″ × 8″ faience tiles which did not need a licence, unlike the more normal 6″ square type, and so a large job such as the boiler rooms at the Gillette factory was completed entirely with faience tiles of this size.

Carter's captured a number of big contracts at this time, many of which were on the industrial or utilitarian side, which built up their economic status and their reputation within the building trade. They tiled a number of pumping stations from Hampton to Bristol and also moved into the new field of atomic power stations such as Sizewell in Suffolk. They developed their established contacts with the food retail trade by completing schemes for Sainsbury (whose shops were formerly tiled by Minton) and Fine Fare, and they also tiled the shops' depots and farms. Similarly, the pre-war contacts and expertise with hotel work meant that in the mid 1950s the contracting unit in London ordered and fixed bathroom and kitchen tiles in hotels in Birmingham, Newcastle and Manchester. Unusual work requiring specialist solutions was also undertaken. One such project was the film processing department at Kodak where everything, including the ventilating ducts, had to be tiled immaculately to eliminate any chance of dust.[15]

Most of these contracts were for utilitarian areas and did not involve design work. However, patterned tiles were needed for the public areas of hotels and shopping centres as well as for the large number of schools, colleges and other local council building undertaken during this period. Carter's made and fixed tiles in schools at Stevenage, Hainault Forest, West Ham, Derby, Scunthorpe and Nottingham, and by the mid 1950s it became clear that the production of such designs needed a larger staff than A. B. Read and Peggy Angus.

In 1955 Ivor Kamlish was appointed as an assistant to A. B. Read and to work solely for the Tileworks. Kamlish had graduated from the Central School in London where he had been taught by Robert Nicholson, a friend of Read's. Kamlish himself had provided some designs for the Tileworks' silk-screening department, notably one known by the Carter employees as the 'barbed wire' pattern[16] which was, as this nickname suggests, a series of vertical lines enlivened along their length with small stars or asterisks. Nicholson recommended Kamlish who was appointed in September 1955. Kamlish's particular training was in graphic and interior design and a final-year project had been on a design showroom for

DOLPHIN SCREEN PRINTED CERAMIC TILES

PR 484

PR 484 shown in repeat

PR 378

PR 378 shown in repeat

PR 521

PR 521 shown in repeat

PR 143

PR 143 shown in repeat

Ivor Kamlish MSIA

Robert Nicholson FSIA

Ivor Kamlish MSIA

A. B. Read RDI FSIA ARCA

Screen-printed tile designs by Ivor Kamlish, Robert Nicholson (the 'barbed wire' design) and A. B. Read. 1958–64. *Illustration: Dolphin Ceramic Tiles Catalogue, 1964.*

Screen-printed tile designs by Ivor Kamlish and A. B. Read. 1958–64. *Illustration: Dolphin Ceramic Tiles Catalogue, 1964.*

a ceramic manufacturer. He contributed to many aspects of Carter design. During his time there he produced patterns for printed tiles as well as several murals of hand-painted tiles. His decorative panels were made for public houses and churches from London to Northampton, from the swimming pool of the *Northern Star*, a Shaw Savill liner, to a supermarket in Peckham Rye. One innovatory design which Kamlish introduced was for a 'textured surface' tile. In this range, to which A. B. Read also contributed, each tile bore a deeply moulded repeat pattern, available in eighty colours for both interior and exterior use.

Using his art school training, Kamlish was also responsible for the graphic side of Carter's image – packaging, leaflets, letter headings, catalogues, etc. – and by the time he left in 1965 his work consisted almost entirely of designs in this field. For the first three years he worked at Poole, but in 1958 he was attached to the London showroom at 44, Bloomsbury Street, where he opened a design unit formed specifically to co-operate with architects. The showroom had previously been at No. 42, and was moved next door in 1953. Other offices were also attached to these premises including David Carter's, Ronald Cole's and A. B. Read's own design studio.[17] Phyllis Habgood was brought up from Poole and Brian Moore joined Carter & Co. (London) in 1959 after training at Poole Art School in painting, fabric design and pottery. He moved to the design unit in 1962.[18] A fourth member, Colin Bowles, joined later, having trained at the Royal College of Art. This group produced designs for all types of work from hand-painted and tubeline decorated tiles to faience and mosaic. The work involved both the use of standard production and the design of special commissions. The unit members and some decorators such as Phyllis Butler, down at Poole, produced many of these designs. Brian Moore, for instance, apart from working on Ivor Kamlish's projects, designed several large projects and murals such as Warwick Road Telephone Exchange, London, in 1961; a glass mosaic for Shell BP at Harlow in about 1965, the design for which was based on the structure of the earth; and the long panel opposite the waiting area at Poole Hospital, in 1967. Each design unit member also collaborated with the others and Brian Moore did several 'full-sizing' drawings for Kamlish such as the one for the *Northern Star* mural. In addition to such staff designers, outside artists were also invited to contribute and these included some

DOLPHIN TEXTURED SURFACE TILES

TS 1

TS 1 shown in repeat

Ivor Kamlish MSIA

TS 2

TS 2 shown in repeat

Ivor Kamlish MSIA

Fireplace designed by Heal & Son Ltd using textured surface tiles TS2

Textured surface tile designs by Ivor Kamlish, showing the moulded relief tiles in use in a fireplace scheme designed by Heal & Son. 1958. *Illustration: Dolphin Ceramic Tiles Catalogue, 1964.*

Screen-printed tile designs by Ivor Kamlish and Gordon Cullen. *c.* 1958.
Illustration: Dolphin Ceramic Tiles Catalogue, 1964.

Screen-printed tile designs by Laurence Scarfe. 1958–60. *Illustration: Dolphin Ceramic Tiles Catalogue, 1964.*

important names such as Gordon Cullen, the architect, and Laurence Scarfe.

As well as these projects for individual firms, Carter's made hand-painted tiles for various authorities, both local, as in the case of a mosaic and tile panel designed by Richard Emett for the new town of Hemel Hempstead, and national, such as the plaques identifying the various species of birds for St James's Park, London, designed by Peter Scott. In these instances it was thought that the designers would paint their own designs, until a demonstration by the Carter paintresses illustrated the special skills and experience necessary. As a result, Phyllis Butler was the paintress who executed both these jobs.[19] Such designs were featured at trade exhibitions throughout the period and the Tileworks continued to commission display stands from contemporary architects as they had done during the 1930s. In addition to the established contact with F. R. S. Yorke, Gordon Cullen was one such architect and A. B. Read's son, Christopher, was another.

Exhibition display was one area in which Carter's demonstrated their policy of promoting production through the best of contemporary design. This was a genuine and deeply held conviction by the Carter family, pursued throughout the company's existence, and in the late 1950s and early 1960s it was further upheld by the use of the imaginative work of the photographer Eric de Maré. De Maré specialized in studies of architectural and other subjects seen from unexpected angles, in such a way as to illustrate formerly unnoticed or unappreciated aspects. Carter's used this talent in a series of stylish advertisements in the *Architects' Journal* and *The Builder*, in which various points in tile production were illustrated with unexpected and eye-catching drama.

In 1958 an international exhibition was held in Brussels and the opportunity arose for Peggy Angus to extend the possibilities of her diagonally halved, printed tiles shown on the Building Trades Exhibition stand in 1951. Carter & Co. produced a mural in which the design explored all the pictorial permutations possible using plain and diagonally patterned tiles relieved with other decorations such as spots or squares. The panel was mounted near water, so that the images repeated across the panel surface were also repeated in the reflection.

Various special commissions were also completed, notably the bathrooms of the Strand Palace Hotel. In 1961 this contract was

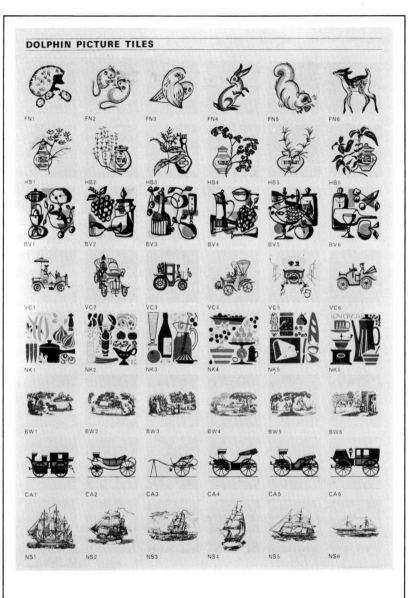

DOLPHIN PICTURE TILES

FN1 FN2 FN3 FN4 FN5 FN6

HB1 HB2 HB3 HB4 HB5 HB6

BV1 BV2 BV3 BV4 BV5 BV6

VC1 VC2 VC3 VC4 VC5 VC6

NK1 NK2 NK3 NK4 NK5 NK6

BW1 BW2 BW3 BW4 BW5 BW6

CA1 CA2 CA3 CA4 CA5 CA6

NS1 NS2 NS3 NS4 NS5 NS6

Printed picture tiles, designed by Sylvia Ball, Una Hart, Margaret Matthews and Daphne Padden. *c.* 1960–64. *Illustration: Dolphin Ceramic Tiles Catalogue, 1964.*

won by Carter's in competition with many other applicants, and they made a series of panels decorated with early prints of the Thames which they reproduced with a waterproof photo-stencil technique, a method which had replaced the earlier one of hand-cutting. Particularly prestigious work in this category of individual commissions was the series of reredoses designed by Joseph Ledger in the mid-1950s and 1960s. The painting for these was done by Phyllis Butler in a special section set up at Poole for the purpose, and they were mounted in the Church of St John Fisher at Rochester and the Church of St Mary the Virgin, Hounslow, both designed around 1955. The architect in each case was H. S. Goodhart–Rendel who at that time particularly favoured tile decoration for its durability and commissioned the designs from Ledger. In 1966 a third reredos was made for the Church of Our Lady of the Rosary in Old Marylebone Road, London, to Ledger's design, although by that time he was in Stoke-on-Trent, working for Doulton.[20] Again the architect was Goodhart-Rendel, who died in 1959, but fortunately he left clear and largely finished drawings for the main building. Completion and execution of the design was carried out by F. G. Broadbent and Partners. The reredos formed the focal point of the interior and the design consisted of fifteen painted tile panels depicting the Mysteries of the Rosary. In addition to the reredos, Carter & Co. were also responsible for providing and fixing the glazed tiling, decorated with a geometrical pattern, to the sanctuary walls up to an ornamental stone band at sill level.[21]

Tile panel, designed by Joseph Ledger for the Pottery Works and mounted on an inside wall. The design was based on the factory production. 1955. *Poole Pottery Ltd.*

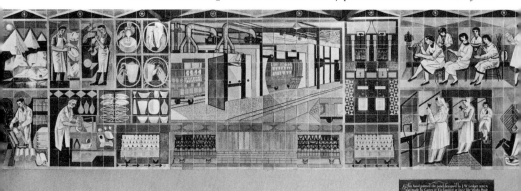

Mosaic facade for flats at Gosport, designed by Kenneth Barden for Wimpey.
1963. *Pilkington Tiles Ltd.*

A more secular Ledger panel, produced in 1955 or 1956, was mounted on an interior wall at the Pottery and shows the production of pottery from the claypit to the making room. Visitors on guided tours were able to view the panel and simultaneously to look down on the Gibbons electric tunnel kiln.

The work of the Tileworks during this decade and a half ranges from war damage repairs to recovering their pre-war status with contracts for the production and fixing of entire tiling schemes and projects. Production increased and a balance was maintained between the vast, industrial projects involving many thousands of plain tiles, and the re-establishment of a continuing contemporary awareness represented by the design unit, which employed both trained designers and, in the time-honoured Poole tradition, a healthy influx of visiting outside artists with varying levels of experience in the media.

On the administrative side, Carter's were not only represented but were frequently instrumental in setting up the various councils concerned with standardization of colours and materials. These moves towards officially recognized levels of manufacture were typical of the industrial climate of the time, when an increasing need for larger production combined with health and other considerations made such developments essential.

Carter's, like many other old established firms, were becoming less and less like the cosy, locally-based community – with a London extension – that they had been before the war. The final break with the old image came in 1963 when Cyril Carter retired and there was no longer a family interest in the company. It was a time when many manufacturers were combining their interests with other firms and in 1964, when Pilkington Tiles Ltd showed such an interest in Carter's, the Board decided to accept their offer.

NOTES

Chapter 1

1. Llewellynn Jewitt, *Ceramic Art of Great Britain*, 1883, pp. 237, 238.
2. Geoffrey Godden, *Encyclopaedia of British Pottery and Porcelain Marks*, 1964.
3. Herbert Carter, *I Call to Mind*, 1949, p. 1. Although Herbert Carter (William Carter's son) specifies a James Walker, the surviving East Quay tiles are marked 'T. W. Walker'; Carter is not always entirely reliable, writing from childhood memories and hearsay rather than first-hand experience. However, T. W. Walker may well have been a close relative whose name was used for legal purposes in the formation of the company.
4. Conversation with Archie H. Hannam, 1 August 1978.
5. Conversation with Bill Eason, 24 September 1978.
6. Charles Carter's unpublished diaries.
7. Herbert Carter, *I Call to Mind*, pp. 5, 21. In the *London Business Directory*, 1878, the Kinson Pottery Co. had its London Office on the Albert Embankment. No number is given but by 1908 Carter & Co. also took up offices on the Albert Embankment, at No. 29. There is no record of this, but they may have taken over offices acquired by William.
8. Charles Carter's unpublished diaries, 17 September 1876, 'Mr Walker prosecuted'.
9. *Littlebury's Directory and Gazetteer of Worcestershire*, 1873.
10. *Kelly's Directory*, Worcestershire section, 1888.
11. Herbert Carter, *I Call to Mind*, p. 16.
12. *The Business Directory of London and Provincial Guide*, 1878.
13. *Ibid.*
14. Letter, 4 March 1880, Wedgwood Archive, Keele University.
15. Charles Carter mentions that Ernest Blake suffered from boils.
16. *Building News*, 2 July 1886, p. 13.
17. *Building News*, 3 June 1887, p. 829, and 23 October 1896, p. 538.
18. The medal is still kept at the Tileworks.
19. *Building News*, 11 September 1891, p. 356, and 4 November 1892, p. 628.
20. Owen Carter, 'On Designing for Tiles', contribution to *Practical Designing, a Handbook on the Preparation of Working Drawings*, ed. Gleeson White, 1893, pp. 103–18.
21. Conversation with James Radley Young, son of the artist, 5 November 1978.
22. Conversation with Bill Eason, 19 September 1977.
23. Roy T. Holland, unpublished memoirs.
24. William J. Furnival, *Leadless Decorative Tiles, Faience and Mosaic*, 1904, p. 197.

Chapter 2

1. Herbert Carter, *I Call to Mind*, 1949, pp. 17, 18. There is some uncertainty as to whether Owen was living at West End House at this time and other addresses at Parkstone have been suggested.
2. Conversation with Donald S. Farmer, 1 September 1978.
3. Conversation with Bill Eason, 29 September 1977.
4. Charles Carter's unpublished diaries.
5. Conversation with Mrs Alice Coward, 25 September 1978.
6. Carter & Co. records.
7. Léon Lefèvre, *Architectural Pottery*, 1900, p. 424.
8. Carter & Co. records.
9. William J. Furnival, *Leadless Decorative Tiles, Faience and Mosaic*, 1904, pp. 196–200.
10. Charles Carter's unpublished diaries, 16 March 1900. 'The girl Brown died – suggestion of lead poisoning', 17 March, 'Inquest on the girl Brown in afternoon, post mortem did not reveal cause of death so it was decided to adjourn inquest for the purpose [of?] the various organs of the body to be analysed.' The rest of this entry has been completely scratched out. 31 March, 'Adjourned inquest on the girl Brown.' These entries are exceptional as Charles' diaries are almost totally concerned with social events – cycling trips (of which there were very many) parties, dances, ping pong games, sailing, photography, magic lantern shows, Natural History Society, Masonic and Council meetings. Comments on the Pottery are generally confined to brief and unhelpful entries such as 'At Pottery all morning', and notes of trains caught to London and Manchester offices, but without any details. There are minimal entries regarding visits to various tileworks such as Maw's and Craven's, H. & R. Johnson, and Dennis's Tileworks at Ruabon, as well as general visits to Stoke, Hanley, Burslem and Tunstall. Return visits were made to Carter & Co. by Maw and Johnson.
11. Carter & Co. records, and *London Street Directory*, 1902. By 1902 Carter's had moved their offices to 43, Essex Street. At this point they shared the accommodation with William Carter's Kinson Pottery; the offices were also shared by the *British Clayworker Trade Journal* and the Institute of Clayworkers. By 1911 Carter's had moved to 29, Albert Embankment.
12. Conversation with Bill Eason, 3 September 1978.
13. *Ibid.*
14. *Ibid.*
15. *Ibid.*
16. *Science and Art Journal for Teachers and Students*, 1892.
17. Conversation with C. J. N. Unwin about his father, 31 August 1978.
18. From an un-named newspaper cutting in Mrs C. J. N. Unwin's possession.
19. Conversation with Bill Eason, 29 September 1978.
20. Conversation with James Radley Young about his father, 5 November 1978.

Chapter 3

1. J. H. Barratt & Co. Ltd became part of the Carter Group in 1928.
2. Conversation with C. J. N. Unwin (W. C. Unwin's son) 31 August 1978 and with James Radley Young (J. R. Y.'s son), 5 November 1978.
3. Conversation with Archie H. Hannam, 1 August 1978.
4. John Adams, 'Potter's Parade No. 17', *Pottery and Glass*, October 1950, p. 55.

5. Conversation with Archie H. Hannam, 1 August 1978.

6. Conversation with Bill Eason, recalling remarks made by his father Alfred Eason, 24 September 1978.

7. Lucien Myers, *The First Hundred Years*, 1973, p. 20.

8. Conversation with Donald S. Farmer, 1 August 1978.

9. Lucien Myers, *The First Hundred Years*, p. 20.

10. Conversation with Miss Dacombe, 14 January 1979. Her father, J. Dacombe, was connected with the Bournemouth committee which arranged accommodation for the refugees when they arrived. Miss Dacombe owns a plate painted in the Delft/Poole technique by Roelants and given by the artist to her father.

11. Virginia Woolf, *Roger Fry*, 1940, p. 188 (extracts from this work quoted in this chapter are reproduced by kind permission of the Author's Literary Estate and The Hogarth Press).

12. *Omega Workshops Ltd*, brochure, *c.* 1915, Preface and p. 10.

13. Richard Shone, unpublished conversation with Miss Winifred Gill.

14. Virginia Woolf, *Roger Fry*, p. 204.

15. *Ibid.*, pp. 204–5.

16. Conversation with Archie H. Hannam, 1 September 1978.

17. *Omega Workshops Ltd*, Preface.

18. Virginia Woolf, *Roger Fry*, p. 239.

19. Conversation with Margaret Holder, 2 August 1978.

20. Conversation with James Radley Young, 5 November 1978.

21. Conversation with Bill Eason, January 1979.

22. Conversation with James Radley Young, 5 November 1978.

23. Conversation with Ronald G. Cole, 1 August 1978.

24. Cyril Carter, *A Report for the Year 1920*, Carter & Co., pp. 3–9, 13, 14.

Chapter 4

1. Cyril Carter, *A Report for the Year 1920*, Carter & Co., pp. 14, 15.

2. Conversation with Ronald G. Cole, 1 August 1978.

3. Conversation with Donald S. Farmer, 1 August 1978.

4. Conversation with David Carter, Cyril Carter's son, 19 September 1978.

5. Michael Farr, *Design in British Industry*, 1955, pp. 192–4, 198, 199.

6. John Adams, 'Potter's Parade No. 18', *Pottery and Glass*, November 1950, p. 58.

7. The Russian Ballet held their first London season in 1911; *L'Après-Midi d'un faune* was first performed in London in 1913. Richard Buckle, *Nijinsky*, 1971, p. 326.

8. John Adams, 'Potter's Parade No. 18', p. 60.

9. *Ibid.*, p. 61.

10. Charles Carter's unpublished diary for 1898, 19 June.

11. Conversation with Margaret Holder, 2 August 1978.

12. Information from Dorothy Mainstone (*née* James), who says that a further eleven paintresses were subsequently employed.

13. Conversation with Ruth Thomson (*née* Pavely), 28 September 1977.

14. Conversation with Ronald G. Cole, 1 August 1978.

15. Conversation with Ruth Thomson, 28 September 1977.

16. Conversation with Margaret Holder, 2 August 1978. In the late 1920s Erna Manners was working independently as a potter from an address in Ealing, London. *Studio Year Book*, 1927, p. 132.

17. Letter from Margaret Holder, 4 August 1978. The photographic records no longer survive.
18. Conversation with Ernest Legg, 13 October 1977.
19. Conversation with Miss B. Bibby, 11 October 1977.
20. B.I.I.A. exhibition, 1924, catalogue.
21. B.I.I.A. exhibition, 1922, 'Present Day Industrial Art', catalogue.
22. B.I.F. exhibition, 1923, catalogue.
23. *Pottery Gazette and Glass Trade Review*, August 1921, p. 1220.
24. *Ibid.*, October 1921, p. 1531.
25. Poole Pottery, catalogue, *c.* 1922, pp. 5, 6.
26. Poole Pottery, catalogue, *c.* 1923, p. 4.
27. Paris, International Exhibition of Modern Decorative and Industrial Art, 1925, catalogue.
28. Michael Farr, *Design in British Industry*, 1955, p. 194.
29. *Pottery Gazette and Glass Trade Review*, April 1926, p. 598.

Chapter 5

1. 'A variety of POOLE POTTERY known as Sylvan Ware', advertising leaflet, *c.* 1935.
2. Conversation with Ernest Baggaley, 24 September 1978.
3. Conversation with David Carter, 19 September 1978.
4. Conversation with Leslie Elsden, October 1977, and Margaret Holder, 2 August 1978. Miss Holder made the original working drawings for this set and also for a second version, the size scaled up with the aid of a proportional compass sent down to her by Harold Stabler from Messrs Nichol, instrument makers.
5. Conversation with Ernest Baggaley, 24 September 1978, and Phyllis Cattle, 22 September 1978.
6. *The Dorset Year Book*, 1941–2, pp. 42–4.
7. Conversation with Margaret Holder, 2 August 1978.
8. *Ibid.*
9. *Ibid.*
10. Information from Miss Brownsword, daughter of the artist.
11. Conversation with Margaret Holder, 2 August 1978.
12. B.I.I.A. exhibition, 'Modern Crafts and Manufacturers', 1920, catalogue introduction.
13. B.I.I.A. exhibition, 'Industrial Art in Relation to the Home', 1933, catalogue.
14. Royal Academy exhibition, 'British Art in Industry', 1935, catalogue.
15. Paris, International Exhibition, 1937, catalogue, pp. 42, 43.

Chapter 6

1. B.I.F. exhibition, 1917, catalogue, pp. 27, 159.
2. *The Builder*, January 1927, p. 84.
3. Conversation with Phyllis Cattle, September 1978, and others. Probably only Castle's feet were used!
4. Conversation with Margaret Holder, 2 August 1978.
5. Conversation with Phyllis Cattle, September 1978.

6. *The Pottery Gazette and Glass Trade Review*, 1 January 1926, pp. 103, 105. According to this article the overall design was by the architect and perspective artist, H. L. G. Pilkington, and Stabler also carried out the modelling for the bronze work as well as the faience.

7. *The Builder*, January 1927, p. 84.

8. Conversation with Margaret Holder, 2 August 1978.

9. The memorial has been boarded up since the last war and is not available for viewing. There is a spare cast of the St George figure in the Poole Pottery Ltd collection.

10. Conversation with Pamela Diamand (*née* Fry), 19 January 1979.

11. Conversation with Margaret Holder, 2 August 1978.

12. Conversation with Bill Eason, 24 September 1978.

13. *Ibid.*

14. Owen Carter, 'On Designing Tiles', contribution to *Practical Designing, a Handbook on the Preparation of Working Drawings*, ed. J. Gleeson White, 1893, pp. 108, 109.

15. Conversation with Bill Eason, 3 August 1978.

16. Conversation with Arthur Nickols, cousin of the artist, 25 January 1979.

17. Conversation with Bill Eason, 3 August 1978.

18. Conversation with Margaret Holder, 2 August 1978.

19. Conversation with Phyllis Butler, 31 August 1978.

20. Conversation with Margaret Holder, 2 August 1978.

21. *Ibid.*

22. *Mac Matters*, Mac Fisheries house journal, No. 4, 1925 (probably June), p. 82.

23. Sydney R. Jones, 'Art and Publicity, Fine Printing and Design', *The Studio*, Special Number, 1925, pp. 77 and 109.

24. Conversation with Leslie Coombe, 1 August 1978.

25. Leslie Elsden remembers J. R. Y. coming to one of these parties dressed as a pirate.

Chapter 7

1. Conversation with Reginald Till, 25 March 1977.

2. International Exhibition of Modern Decorative and Industrial Art, Paris, 1925, catalogue, Grand Palais section.

3. The design is now in the collections of the Victoria and Albert Museum.

4. Conversation with Bill Eason, 3 August 1978.

5. Conversation with Jim Allen, 2 August 1978.

6. John Gloag, *The Architect and Building News*, 8 January 1932, pp. 35–43, and *Supplement, The Architect Portfolio*, No. 158.

7. *The Architects' Journal*, 29 May 1929, pp. 821–8.

8. *The Builder*, 5 July 1929, p. 27.

9. *The Architects' Journal*, 29 May 1929, p. 826.

10. *The Builder*, 26 February 1932, pp. 386, 389–91, 396.

11. Conversation with Ronald G. Cole, February 1979.

12. *The Builder*, 20 December 1935, pp. 110, 118.

13. Tim Benton, 'The De La Warr Pavilion, a type for the 1930s', *Leisure in the Twentieth Century*, Design Council, 1977, pp. 72–80.

14. Conversation with David Carter, Cyril Carter's son, October 1978.

15. Conversation with Margaret Holder, 2 August 1978.

16. *The Builder*, 28 June 1935, p. 1202.

17. *The Builder*, 9 August 1935, pp. 232, 250; *Carter, Picture Tiles for Hospitals*, Carter & Co. Ltd, 1935.
18. Conversation with Margaret Holder, 2 August 1978.
19. *Architectural Review*, September 1933, p. 116.
20. *Architectural Review*, May 1933, Supplement, p. 213.
21. Letters from Carter & Co. Ltd to W. B. Honey, 15 February 1939.
22. Conversation with Ronald G. Cole, 1 August 1978.
23. Letter from W. B. Honey to Harold Stabler, 9 February 1939.
24. Conversation with Donald S. Farmer, 1 August 1978.
25. Carter & Co. Ltd records.
26. Conversation with Ronald G. Cole, 1 August 1978.
27. *Ibid.*

Chapter 8

1. Harry Trethowan, 'Utility Pottery', *The Studio*, vol. 125, 1943, pp. 48, 49.
2. Roy T. Holland, unpublished memoirs.
3. Conversation with Mrs A. A. Carter (Mrs Cyril Carter), 25 August 1978.
4. Conversation with Ernest Baggaley, 24 September 1978, and with Phyllis Cattle, September 1978.
5. Conversation with Ernest Baggaley, 24 September 1978.
6. Poole Pottery Ltd records.
7. Roy T. Holland, unpublished memoirs.
8. *Pottery and Glass*, June 1950, p. 37.
9. *Ibid.*, Lucien Myers, 'The First Hundred Years', 1973, p. 32, and *Poole Pottery, Descriptive Brochure*, 1950.
10. Poole Pottery Ltd records.
11. Roy T. Holland, unpublished memoirs.
12. Poole Pottery Ltd records.
13. *Pottery Gazette and Glass Trade Review*, September 1951, p. 1400.
14. *Festival of Britain*, 1951, H.M.S.O., catalogue of exhibits.
15. Conversations with Mrs A. B. Read, 13 January 1979, and Ann Tibbey (*née* Read), same date. Despite this early dating these tiles did not appear in a Carter & Co. Ltd catalogue until 1939 when they were described as 'offered now for the first time'.
16. Conversation with Mrs A. B. Read, 13 January 1979.
17. Poole Pottery Ltd records.
18. *Pottery Gazette and Glass Trade Review*, April 1953, p. 570.
19. *Pottery Gazette and Glass Trade Review*, July 1958, contents page.
20. Conversation with Ann Tibbey (*née* Read), 13 January 1979.
21. Conversation with Mrs A. B. Read, 13 January 1979.
22. Buller's studio was in operation between 1934 and 1952. *Art Among the Insulators*, exhibition catalogue, 1977.
23. Conversation with Robert Jefferson, 14 January 1979.
24. *Ibid.*
25. *Pottery Gazette and Glass Trade Review*, July 1962, pp. 838, 839.
26. *Ibid.* and Roy T. Holland's unpublished memoirs.
27. *Pottery Gazette and Glass Trade Review*, February 1961, pp. 267–9.
28. Conversation with Robert Jefferson, 14 January 1979.

Chapter 9

1. Conversation with Leslie Coombe, 1 August 1978.
2. Conversation with Bill Eason, 29 August 1977.
3. Conversation with Bill Innes, 5 April 1979.
4. The Carter Group, *Carter Quarterly*, November 1951.
5. This work has recently been transferred to Poole Pottery Ltd.
6. *Carter Quarterly*, November 1951, p. 4.
7. Conversation with Leslie Coombe, 1 August 1978.
8. *Carter Mosaic*, brochure, *c.* 1955.
9. *Ibid.*
10. Conversation with Ivor Kamlish, 26 January 1979.
11. Conversation with Peggy Angus, 20 February 1978.
12. *Festival of Britain*, H.M.S.O., catalogue of exhibits.
13. Conversation with Bill Innes and Don Slade, 5 April 1979.
14. *Design*, May–June 1951, p. 23.
15. Conversation with Bill Innes and Don Slade, 5 April 1979.
16. Conversation with Jim Allen, 2 August 1978.
17. David Carter remained on the Board until 1955.
18. Conversation with Brian Moore, 30 April 1979.
19. Conversation with Phyllis Butler, 1 August 1978, and Bill Innes, 5 April 1979.
20. Conversation with Joseph Ledger, 1977 and 10 May 1979.
21. *Building*, 4 March 1966, pp. 113–17.

APPENDIX 1

The Carter Family

ALFRED
Born: 1849   Died: ?
Not working for family firm
Founder of Carter, Brockley

ARTHUR OWEN
Born: 1874   Died: 1956
Working: *c*. 1900–49
Carter & Co. (London)
Also, founder of Carter & Sons,
Vauxhall

CHARLES
Born: 1860   Died: 1934
Working: 1877–*c*. 1930
Director/Chairman

CHARLES CYRIL
Born: 1888   Died: 1969
Working: 1904–65
Chairman

DAVID
Born: 1913
Working: 1939–59
Director, Poole Pottery and
Carter & Co.

ERNEST BLAKE
Born: 1856   Died: 1883
Working: 1881–3
London office, accounts

HARRY
Born: 1890   Died: 1960
Not working for family firm
Twin brother of Roger

HERBERT SPENCER
Born: 1880   Died: 1956
Not working for family firm
Author of *I Call to Mind*, autobiography

JESSE
Born: 1830   Died: 1926
Working: 1873–*c*. 1889
although he continued in an
advisory capacity for many
years
Founder

OWEN
Born: 1862   Died: 1919
Working: 1877–1919
Art Director

ROGER
Born: 1890   Died: 1959
Working: *c*. 1914–29
London office and sales, time and
motion study at Tileworks
Twin brother of Harry

APPENDIX 2

Technicians, artists, designers
and other workers

An asterisk indicates people interviewed by the author.

A D A M S, John, A.R.C.A.
Born: 1882 Died: 1953
Working at C.S.A.: 1921–50
Managing Director
Shape design and glaze development, stonewares, Streamline tableware

* A L L E N, Jim
Born: 1911
Working at Carter & Co. (Tiles): 1929–76
Printed tiles, silk-screening

* A N G U S, Peggy
Born: ?
Working, freelance, for Carter & Co. (Tiles): 1949/50–1960
Tile design

* B A G G A L E Y, Ernest
Born: 1904
Working at C.S.A.: 1936–45
Works Manager
Glaze development and shape design

* B A R R I N G T O N, George
Born: 1923
Working at Carter & Co. (Tiles): 1937 to the present day
Director
Floor tiles

B A T T Y, Dora M.
Born: ?
Working, freelance, for C.S.A. and Carter & Co. (Tiles): *c.* 1921–5
Pattern design, children's wares, graphic work

* B A W D E N, Edward
Born: 1903
Working, freelance, for C.S.A. and Carter & Co. (Tiles): *c.* 1922 and 1961
Graphic work, tile and mosaic design

B E L L, Vanessa
Born: 1879   Died: 1961
Working for the Omega Workshops, possibly at Carter & Co.:
c. 1914–18
Pottery decoration

* B I B B Y, Beatrice
Born: ?
Working at C.S.A.: 1922–38
Secretarial work with John Adams

B O U R N E, Olive
Born: ?
Working, freelance, for C.S.A.: *c.* 1930
Pattern design

B O W L E S, Colin
Born: ?
Working at Carter & Co. (Tiles): *c.* 1958–?
Design

B R A D B U R Y, Arthur Royce
Born: 1894   Died: 1977
Working, freelance, for C.S.A.: *c.* 1932–5
Designs for ship plates

B R O W N, Harry
Born: ?   Died: *c.* 1960
Working for Carter & Co.: *c.* 1918–*c.* 1956
Sculptural faience

B R O W N S W O R D, Harold, A.R.C.A.
Born: ?
Working, freelance, for C.S.A.: *c.* 1921–35
Figure design

* B U T L E R, Phyllis
Born: 1912
Working at Carter & Co. (Tiles): 1927–72
Tile painting department and design

C A R S O N, Phyllis, (*née* Habgood)
Born: ?
Working for Carter & Co. (Tiles): ?
Tile painting Poole, and design unit in London

C A R T E R, Truda (Gertrude), (*née* Sharp)
Born: 1890   Died: 1958
Working at C.S.A.: 1921–5?

* C A T T L E, Phyllis, (*née* Way)
Born: 1914
Working at C.S.A.: 1928–75
Showroom sales

* C O L E, Ronald George
Born: 1906
Working at Carter & Co. and Carter & Co. (London): 1920–68
Director and Managing Director
Drawing office and contracts department

* C O O M B E, Leslie
Born: 1908
Working at Carter & Co. (Tiles): 1924–73
Drawing office and mosaic department

* C O W A R D, Alice, (*née* Woodland)
Born: 1896
Working at Carter & Co.: *c.* 1914–18
Lustre glazing and tile cleaning

C U L L E N, T. Gordon
Born: 1914
Working, freelance, for Carter & Co. (Tiles): *c.* 1958–60
Exhibition stand and tile design

D R A W B E L L, Marjorie
Born: ?
Working, freelance, for C.S.A.: late 1930s and 1949
Animal figure design

E A S O N, Alfred John
Born: 1854   Died: 1921
Working at Carter & Co.: 1888–1921 (?)
Development of ceramic marble, glaze development

* E A S O N, William
Born: 1894
Working at Carter & Co. (Tiles): 1909–60
Faience department, drawing office

E L F O R D, Benjamin Evelyn
Born: ?
Working at Carter & Co.: 1898 (or earlier) –1947
Company Secretary, Managing Director, Chairman

E L L I S, Clifford
Born: ?   Died: ?
Working briefly with Carter & Co. (Tiles): 1935
Design for mosaic panel shown in exhibition 'British Art in Industry',
Royal Academy, 1935

E L L I S, Rosemary
Born: ?   Died: ?
Co-designer and wife of Clifford, above

* E L S D E N, Leslie
Born: 1912
Working at C.S.A.: 1926 to the present day
Spraying shop and design department, Picotee, Aegean ranges, etc.

F A R L E I G H, John
Born: 1900   Died: 1965
Working, freelance, for Carter & Co. (Tiles): 1935
Design for faience panel, shown in the exhibition 'British Art in
Industry', Royal Academy, 1935

* F A R M E R, Donald Service
Born: 1902
Working at Carter & Co. (Tiles): 1920–71
Glaze chemistry, Wall Tile works

F A W K E S, Irene
Born: ?
Working, freelance, for C.S.A.: *c.* 1925–30
Pattern design and graphic work

F R Y, Roger
Born: 1866   Died: 1934
Working for the Omega Workshops, at Carter & Co.: 1914–18
Shape design

G I L H A M, Gertie (Gertrude)
Born: 1902   Died: 1974
Working for C.S.A.: 1916–50
Throwing

G I L H A M, Lily
Born: 1897   Died: 1968
Working for Carter & Co. and C.S.A.: 1914–23
Tile decoration, modelling and throwing

* H A N N A M, Archie H.
Born: 1899
Working for Carter & Co.: 1913–61
Accounts and Company Secretary

* H O L L A N D, Roy T.
Born: 1911
Working at C.S.A.: 1945–76
Works Manager, Managing Director

*J E F F E R S O N, Robert, A.R.C.A.
Born: 1929
Working at C.S.A.: 1958–66
Shape and decoration design, Contour, Compact, oven-to-table ware, Studio wares, etc.

*K A M L I S H, Ivor
Born: 1931
Working at Carter & Co. (Tiles): 1955–65
Tile design, graphic work, design unit in London

*L E D G E R, Joseph
Born: 1926
Working with Carter & Co. (Tiles): 1951–54/5 and *c.* 1966
Tile panel design, special commissions, reredoses, etc.

*L E G G, Ernest
Born: 1906
Working at Carter & Co. (Tiles): 1920–23, 1950–57
Working at C.S.A.: 1923–41
Glaze making

M A N N E R S, Erna
Born: ?
Working, freelance, for C.S.A.: *c.* 1921–5
Pattern design (Grapes and Fuschia designs)

*M O O R E, Brian
Born: 1938
Working at Carter & Co. (Tiles): *c.* 1958–63/4
Design, design unit in London

*M O R R I S, Tony
Born: 1942
Working at Carter & Co. (Tiles) and C.S.A.: 1963 to the present day
Faience and pattern/decoration design, Studio and Delphis ranges, etc.

M Y E R S, Lucien
Born: 1903
Working at C.S.A.: 1949–62
Managing Director, some pattern design

N I C H O L S O N, Robert
Born: ?
Working, freelance, for Carter & Co. (Tiles): *c.* 1955
Tile design

N I C K O L S, Arthur
Born: 1894   Died: 1976
Working at Carter & Co. (Tiles): 1920–65
Tile panels and drawing office, 'Dolphin and Kiln' symbol

R E A D, Alfred Burgess, A.R.C.A., R.D.I.
Born: 1898   Died: 1973
Working at Carter & Co. (Tiles) and C.S.A.: *c.* 1923–4, 1951–5, 1957–8
Pattern and shape design, design unit in Poole and London

* R E A D, Ann, (Mrs Tibbey)
Born: 1926
Working at Carter & Co. (Tiles) and C.S.A.: 1952–6
Pattern design and decoration

R O E L A N T S, Joseph
Born: ?
Working at Carter & Co.: *c.* 1918
Tile design and in-glaze technique development

S C A R F E, Laurence
Born: 1914
Working, freelance, for Carter & Co. (Tiles): *c.* 1960
Tile design

S T A B L E R, Harold, A.R.C.A.
Born: 1872   Died: 1945
Working at C.S.A.: 1921– *c.* 1939
Director, faience design and sculpture (Durban and Rugby War
Memorials, etc.), tile design (Waterbirds, etc.) small figure and shaɔe
design

S T A B L E R, Phoebe, A.R.C.A.
Born: ?   Died: 1955
Working at C.S.A.: 1921 – early-to-mid-1930s
Faience design (war memorials), small figure design

S T I C K L A N D, E.E.
Born: ?
Working at Carter & Co. (Tiles): *c.* 1921–30
Tiles design (Farmyard)

* T I L L, Reginald
Born: 1895   Died: 1978
Working at Carter & Co. (Tiles): 1923–51
Faience and tile design and development, silk-screening

T U R N E R, Edwin Page
Born: *c.* 1860   Died: ?
Working at Carter & Co.: pre 1893–1904
Tile panel painting and design

U N W I N, William Carter
Born: 1894   Died: 1935
Working at Carter & Co.: 1896– *c.* 1919/20
Sculpture department

Y O U N G, James Radley
Born: 1867   Died: 1933
Working at Carter & Co.: 1893 – *c.* 1933
Tile panel painting, faience and design department

APPENDIX 3

Paintresses' and decorators' marks

An asterisk indicates people interviewed by the author.
Other marks are verified either directly or indirectly by letter or brief conversation.

A T K I N S , Margaret, (Mrs Stagg)
Born: ?
Working at C.S.A.: *c.* 1922–4

B A R R A T T , Ethel
Born: ?
Working at C.S.A.: *c.* 1924–40

B A T T, Marjorie, (Mrs Hayward)
Born: 1911
Working at C.S.A.: 1926–35
See also C O L L E T, Winifred

B I S H T O N, Nellie, (Mrs Blackmore)
Born: 1909
Working at C.S.A.: 1927–32, 1944–76

B O N D, Myrtle
Born: ?
Working at C.S.A.: *c.* 1929–42

B R I D L E, Vera
Born: 1908
Working at C.S.A.: 1924–34

B U R G E, Grace, (Mrs Parnaby)   **X**
Born: 1908
Working at C.S.A.: 1926–9

C O L L E T, Winifred   **III**
Born: ?
Working at C.S.A.: *c.* 1923–?
See also B A T T, Marjorie

C O W A R D, Freda   **¢**
Born: ?
Working at C.S.A.: ?

*E L S D E N, Leslie   **I:I**
Born: 1912
Working at C.S.A.: 1926 to the present day
Head of spraying shop
See also list of designers (Appendix 2)

G O U G H, Ruth, (Mrs Heath)   **Q**
Born: 1913
Working at C.S.A.: 1928–34

H A L L E T T, Gladys, (Mrs Hayton)   **Ċ**
Born: 1916
Working at C.S.A.: 1932–41

H A M P T O N, Hilda, (Mrs Cleal)   **X X**
Born: 1911
Working at C.S.A.: 1928–45

H A S K I N S, Gwen, (Mrs Lynch)   **X**
Born: 1924
Working at C.S.A.: 1938–77

H A T C H A R D, Anne, (Mrs Milnthorpe)   **AH**
Born: 1905   Died: 1973
Working at C.S.A.: 1918–36

H A Y E S, Rene, (Mrs Harvey)   **%**
Born: 1910
Working at C.S.A.: 1924–49

*H O L D E R, Margaret (Peggy)
Born: 1900
Working at C.S.A.: 1921–41
1, used occasionally on drawings and possibly on pots:
2, used around 1930:
3, used 1921–late 1920s and late 1930s:
Head of painting department, pre-Second World War

J A M E S, Dorothy, (Mrs Mainstone)
Born: 1910
Working at C.S.A.: 1924–35

*J E F F E R S O N, Robert
Born: 1929
Working at C.S.A.: 1958–66
See also list of designers (Appendix 2)

L U C A S, Christine, (Mrs Neale)
Born: 1921
Working at C.S.A.: 1936–40

M A R S H A L L, Doris, (Mrs Atkins)
Born: 1912
Working at C.S.A.: 1926–36

M I L E S, Audrey
Born: 1923
Working at C.S.A.: 1938–41

*M O R R I S, Tony
Born: 1942
Working at C.S.A.: 1963 to the present day
See also list of designers (Appendix 2)

N U N N S, Sue, (Mrs Russel)
Born: 1933
Working at C.S.A.: 1950 to the present day

*P A V E L Y, Ruth, (Mrs Thomson)
Born: 1903   Died: 1979
Working at C.S.A.: 1922–65
1, used 1922 to before 1935:
2, used from about 1935:
Head of painting department, post-Second World War

P E N N E Y, Sylvia
Born: 1943
Working at C.S.A.: 1960–66

P R A N G N E L L, Eileen, (Mrs Chennell)
Born: 1908
Working at C.S.A.: 1924–37
See also S U M M E R S, Pat

*R E A D, Ann, (Mrs Tibbey)
Born: 1926
Working at Carter & Co. (Tiles) and C.S.A.: 1952–6
See also list of designers (Appendix 2)

R I V E R S, Gertrude, (Mrs Mordue)
Born: 1910
Working at C.S.A.: *c.* 1924–32

R Y A L L, Phyllis, (Mrs Randell)
Born: 1911
Working at C.S.A.: 1928–37

S U M M E R S, Pat
Born: 1934
Working at C.S.A.: 1949 to the present day
See also P R A N G N E L L, Eileen

W A Y, Phyllis, (Mrs Cattle) used 1928–34:
Born: 1914
Working at C.S.A: 1928–75
See also list of other workers (Appendix 2)

W H I F F E N, Ann
Born: ?
Working at C.S.A.: ?

Poole Pottery:
Craft Section Identification Marks

Design

Elaine Williamson
Tony Morris
Leslie Elsden
Ros Sommerfelt
Pat Summers

Throwing

Alan White
Paul Dean
Chris White
Deborah McCutchion
Mandy Norton

Traditional

Karen Hickisson
Janice Dowding
Susan Russell
Carolyn Davies
Johanna Allin

Aegean

Carolyn Wills
Faith Hole
Laura Wills
Karen Ryall
Donna Brogan

Olympus

Jacki Leonard
Julie Miller

Delphis

Tina Fancy

Faience

Cynthia Bennett
Hilda Smith

Stoneware	plate signature	stamp
Linda Garwood		
Elaine Martin		
Eunice Menke		
Lesley Presswood		
Joanna Durant		
Debbie Leroy		
Mary Elliot		
Julia Mabey		
Lindsay Loader		
Sarah Spreadbury		
Janet Abrey		
June Henderson-Don		
Carmen Levo		
Hazel Jones		
Janet Stone		
Jane Freeborn		
Susan Dipple		
Diane Lake		

Stoneware Design

Barbara Linley Adams

APPENDIX 4

Pottery marks

C.S.A. backstamps incised, impressed, painted and, from 1952, printed.
Shape numbers incised (numbers only).
Pattern codes painted (letters only).
Paintresses' insignias painted.
Glaze codes printed (letters and numbers combined).

Impressed or incised from about
1900-20 on pottery

1902–7

Rarely used,
between
1900–8

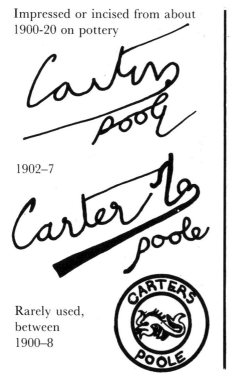

Impressed 1925–52
Excluding 'Ltd.' 1921–4

Impressed or printed, with
or without border lines   1925–78

Impressed mark,
rarely used
1921–5 or later

POOLE
ENGLAND

Painted mark
used on stonewares
c. 1922–35

POOLE

Poole

Impressed mark,
rarely used
1921–*c.* 1925

PRINTED MARKS FROM 1952

1952–5

In one size   In two sizes

1955–9
In three sizes

1959–66   1966
In three sizes   In three sizes

1969–73

Ovenware
October 1960
In three
sizes

POST 1970 MARKS

January 1972

Cameo
Twintone
Compact
Children's Sets
(except mugs)
Ovenware

Morocco

216

Desert Song

Articles too small to take correct stamp, i.e. Coffee Cups

Stoneware (Lapis)

January 1973

Tableware and Traditional painted ware

Craft ware/ Studio production Aegean (with shape No.) Delphis (with shape No.) Traditional (with shape No.) Dolphin Range (Brooch not stamped)

In two sizes

Decorated Tableware

ENGLAND MOROCCO

Decorated Tableware

Fancies   Party Dishes and
                 Hors d'oeuvres

Toast Racks, Shells, Peppers and Salts
Lamps
Atlantis

POOLE
ENGLAND

June 1974

Tableware, plain and decorated, and Traditional painted ware

January 1976

Contour, Compact and Traditional ware

Broadstone and Parkstone patterned flatware. 'Cyclamen' (Broadstone) and 'Lagoon' (Parkstone) backstamps similar to, but larger than,'Vortex' and 'Arden'

BROADSTONE "SHERWOOD"

PARKSTONE "ARGOSY"

BROADSTONE

"VORTEX"

PARKSTONE

"ARDEN"

Craft ware/ Studio production In three sizes

August 1978

Tableware (Diamond pattern below indicates glaze sprayer's identity.)

Traditional ware

Craftware/ Studio production In three sizes

BIBLIOGRAPHY

Published Sources

B A R N A R D, Julian, *Victorian Ceramic Tiles*, Studio Vista, London, 1972.

B E N T O N, Tim, 'The De La Warr Pavilion, a type for the 1930s', contribution to *Leisure in the Twentieth Century*, Design Council, London, 1977.

C A R T E R, Charles Cyril, *A Report for the Year 1920*, Carter & Co., Curwen Press, London, 1920.

C A R T E R, Herbert Spencer, *I Call to Mind*, J. Looker, Poole, 1949.

C A R T E R, Owen, 'On Designing for Tiles', contribution to *Practical Designing, a Handbook on the Preparation of Working Drawings*, ed. J. Gleeson White, Geo. Bell & Sons, London, 1893.

C A R T E R & C O., Records.

C A R T E R & C O. (L O N D O N), Records.

F A R R, Michael, *Design in British Industry, A Mid-Century Survey*, Cambridge University Press, 1955.

F R Y, Roger, *Letters of Roger Fry*, ed. Denys Sutton, Chatto & Windus, London, 1972.

F R Y, Roger, *Omega Workshops Ltd, Artist Decorators*, brochure, London, 1915.

F U R N I V A L, William J, *Leadless Decorative Tiles, Faience and Mosaic*, W. J. Furnival, Stone, Staffs., 1904.

G A U N T, William and C L A Y T O N - S T A M M, M. D. E., *William De Morgan*, Studio Vista, London, 1971.

G I R O U A R D, Mark, *Victorian Pubs*, Studio Vista, London, 1975.

G O D D E N, Geoffrey, *Encylopaedia of British Pottery and Porcelain Marks*, Barrie & Jenkins, London, 1964.

J E W I T T, Llewellynn, *Ceramic Art of Great Britain*, J. S. Virtue & Co., London, 1878, revised edition 1883.

L A M B T O N, Lucinda, *Vanishing Victoriana*, Phaidon, Oxford, 1976.
L E F Ê V R E, Léon, *Architectural Pottery*, Scott, Greenwood & Co., London, 1900.
M Y E R S, Lucien, *The First Hundred Years*, Poole Pottery Ltd, Poole, 1973.
P O O L E   P O T T E R Y   L T D, Records.
S H O N E, Richard, *Bloomsbury Portraits*, Phaidon, Oxford, 1976.
V I C T O R I A   &   A L B E R T   M U S E U M, *The Poole Potteries*, exhibition catalogue, H.M.S.O., London, 1978.
W O O L F, Virginia, *Roger Fry*, Hogarth Press, London, 1940.

Journals

The Architect & Building News
Architects' Journal
Architectural Review
The Art Journal
The Builder
The Building News
The Business Directory of London & Provincial Guide
The Dorset Year Books (1941–2)
Kelly's Post Office London Directories
Kelly's Directory, Worcestershire Section
Littlebury's Directory & Gazetteer of Worcestershire, 1873
Mac Matters, 1925, (Mac Fisheries House Journal)
Poole & South Western Herald
Pottery Gazette & Glass Trade Review
Pottery & Glass
The Studio (monthly and yearly issues)
Studio, Special Number, 'Art and Publicity, Fine Printing and Design', 1925
International and national industrial and trade exhibition catalogues throughout the period

Unpublished Sources

C A R T E R   &   C O., Records.
C A R T E R   &   C O . (L O N D O N), Records.
C A R T E R, Charles, Diaries, various years from 1876–1930.
H O L L A N D, Roy T., Memoirs.
P O O L E   P O T T E R Y   L T D, Records.

INDEX